BEN HOGAN'S

MAGICAL
DEVICE

THE REAL SECRET TO HOGAN'S SWING
FINALLY REVEALED

TED HUNT

Skyhorse Publishing

Skyhorse Publishing books may be purchased in bulk at special discounts for sales promotion, corporate gifts, fund-raising, or educational purposes. Special editions can also be created to specifications. For details, contact the Special Sales Department, Skyhorse Publishing, 307 West 36th Street, 11th Floor, New York, NY 10018 or info@skyhorsepublishing.com.

Skyhorse® and Skyhorse Publishing® are registered trademarks of Skyhorse Publishing, Inc.®, a Delaware corporation.

Visit our website at www.skyhorsepublishing.com.

10 9 8 7 6 5 4 3 2 1

Paperback ISBN: 978-1-62087-568-1

Library of Congress Cataloging-in-Publication Data

Hunt, Ted.
Ben Hogan's magical device : the real secret to Hogan's swing fi nally revealed / Ted Hunt.
p. cm.
ISBN 978-1-60239-700-2
1. Swing (Golf) 2. Hogan, Ben, 1912-1997. I. Title.
GV979.S9H865 2009
796.352'3--dc22

2009001199

Printed in China

To Canadian golfers Stan Leonard, Moe Norman, George Knudson, Mike Weir, Dick Zokol, and those others who aspire to excellence.

CONTENTS

Golf is a private journey taken with friends over some of the most beautiful scenery on God's green earth, and if you can make a bit of money along the way, the sojourn is all the sweeter. Here Ben Hogan stands beside Jay Hebert, Toby Lyons, and Sam Urzetta. Hebert and Lyons defeated Hogan and Urzetta at Moon Brook Country Club, Jamestown, New York, in 1953, just before The Open at Carnoustie.

INTRODUCTION

If you're a professional touring player, no doubt you already do all or most of the effective things discussed in detail in this book. Perhaps you discovered them the way Ben Hogan did, through years of trial and error. Or perhaps you are of the "new breed" who have enjoyed experience-filled university programs. But when suddenly all the chips are on the table—your chips— and you miss a key shot, what then? Gary Player and Arnold Palmer could be seen "giving themselves little lessons" after a not-so-satisfying shot. This book presents a structure to draw on, plus a couple of stroke-saver suggestions here and there that will get your own imagination going. Besides, there is a lot of good history in here with enough golf stories to show you from whence comes the prize money you make. And wouldn't you really like to know what the secret to Hogan's swing is once and for all so that you can use it, or at least explain it?

If you're a teaching professional, you'll find new ways to forget the band-aids, and introduce your clients to a guiding system that will work for them in putting, chipping, and bunker play, as well as the full shot.

If you're an amateur with a yen to improve your game so that you are breaking eighty regularly, but you also have a career ladder to climb, welcome. This is the place to be.

(Courtesy of Jay Hebert)

The impact zone for Ben Hogan's swing—the focus of this book.

PREFACE

I first met Sean Connery in 1984 at the Bing Crosby National Pro-Am, where real life was suspended for one week during an athletic fantasy on three world-renowned courses loved by Ben Hogan: Pebble Beach, Spyglass Hill, and Cypress Point. The original James Bond of the silver screen was the first and only person with whom I discussed this book before proposing it for publication. He liked parts of the first stuttering rough draft presented over the phone between Vancouver and Nassau, and was gracious enough to suggest that it had helped him. Connery, who resembled Hogan in so many ways—especially in terms of focus on the game of golf and on business professionalism—also had enough mawkish humor to predict that "Mr. Hogan might be pirouetting in his grave."

The possible truth of this suggestion forces me to introduce myself to you in order to demonstrate any credentials that might explain, or at least give credence to, why an amateur golfer like myself would have enough arrogance to write a book defining

Ben Hogan's "Magical Device" and describe in detail how to use "the secret" within it.

As most golfers know, Ben Hogan allegedly had a secret that enabled him to eliminate trouble on the left side of the fairway by hitting a repeating power fade, and this action enabled him to become the most respected, yet misunderstood, competitor on the Professional Golf Tour in the forties and fifties.

Hogan off-handedly referred to his hidden move in his world-famous book, *Five Lessons: The Modern Fundamentals of Golf*. *Life* magazine persuaded him to feature an expanded version in their August 8, 1955 issue. The ensuing difficulty in understanding Hogan's review, however, revealed that top golfers do not necessarily know how to impart explanations for the skills they perform so masterfully on the course. Furthermore, the scribes they employ to ghostwrite their thoughts might not themselves understand the intricacies of the golf swing as an exercise in applied physics, nor do they always describe the applicable maneuvers accurately, using universally understood terms.

As a result, there remains confusion over how Hogan actually applied his secret. Expert after expert has added to the lengthy list of what they think the secret is, but none have been able to explain how it is done.

Having studied and participated in golf for fifty years, I was disappointed to discover that many professional golfers, as instructors, were unable to answer questions concerning the correct application of golf-swing nuances. It occurred to me that the lessons I learned in three years as a professional football player with the BC Lions of the Canadian Football League could also be applied to golf. Football is a quasi-militaristic game that has nearly two hundred years of history from which to teach the precision and timing of strategy that looks so chaotic at first glance. I was a raw rookie, hired because I was a home town boy who had demonstrated the basic skills of catching, kicking, and tackling from rugby, and who had experienced the heat of battle in international victories over Japan, Australia, United States, and the British Lions. And so, without too much hesitation, I signed a four-thousand-dollar contract so that I could: (a) marry Helen, an Olympic swimmer and world record holder in the 100-meter freestyle, and the first Canadian woman to win gold internationally at the Pan-American games in Mexico City; and (b) continue our studies at the University of British Columbia. (You could go a long way on that kind of money in the late fifties and early sixties.)

In football I experienced the kind of coaching not yet widely available in golf, and therefore realized that performance analysis was not only possible, but that it also produced impressive results. Along the way, I took courses in kinesiology and applied physics, and saw how they were put into practice so effectively on the gridiron. When I examined what I had learned in football with Dr. Max Howell, the former international rugby player and analyst from Australia, we were able to change the face of rugby—in Vancouver at least. We won a previously unobtainable number of international victories through the sixties and seventies, to the high point where British Columbia beat the British Lions—a team made up of the best players from England, Scotland, Wales, and both Irelands. To this day, no other Provincial team can say that.

By then, I realized that I had had close and highly focused experience with people who could analyze and teach athletic skills at high and intricate levels, and, after twenty-five years of teaching school and coaching athletics, that I might be one of them. Furthermore, I had been writing professionally for many years, mostly historiography and golf-magazine cover features, but writing nevertheless.

I also remembered that I had degrees in Physiology, Human Kinetics, and a Doctorate in History, with published research, so I became determined to track down Hogan's secret because, although I could hit the ball a long way sometimes, I never really had control. I could kick a rugby ball with draws and fades along different trajectories, but I couldn't tell you where my four iron was going.

I began by reviewing most of the literature concerned with the amazing Ben Hogan and interviewed many professionals (Jack Nicklaus, Cory Pavin, Stan Leonard, Alvie Thompson, Moe Norman, Ernie Brown, George Knudson, and others) who knew him and who had studied his techniques.

The result of my early research produced a clearer understanding of the source of the confusion concerning Hogan's secret. I conceived and tested a hypothesis and was pleased to discover that my analysis stood up to critical examination. But more importantly, my golf game responded with more accurate shots and lower scores, which included shooting my age several times within weeks of embracing the secret. I also discovered that the Magical Device could be applied by the average golfer to putting, chipping, and sand play, as well as full shots. Even if golfers could capture only the bare essence of Ben Hogan's secret, their game would improve markedly. Maybe Mr. Hogan was correct when he predicted that amateur golfers could break eighty with just a little insight. Certainly, aspiring young golfers with strength and potential would benefit from many of Hogan's techniques.

As a result, I offer this book to tell you, with stories and illustrations, a readable explanation of what Ben Hogan's Magical Device is and the foundations that support its successful execution. I will also impart to you Hogan's secret move within—which amazingly enough has three subtle points buried inside the secret. No wonder it was so hard to find.

Interspersed throughout the text are stories from professional acquaintances who spoke with me about their times with Mr. Hogan, and from them I was able to define the anatomical maneuvers they described in slang terms. It then became my task to spell the jargon out in universally understandable terms.

I have had a wonderful time with golf over the years and am surprised to note how many seasons have slipped by, just as I have learned how to shoot my age or better with an expectation of doing it regularly. I finally found out how to play this game by collecting and piecing together the parts that explain in detail Ben Hogan's Magical Device—and his secret, as people call it. The secret was so elusive and yet, like many complex things, it is amazingly simple and very effective.

As a boy I caddied for Dunc Sutherland, the professional at Point Grey Golf Club in Vancouver, who taught me the Scottish style he had learned in Tain, his birthplace. With this free-wheeling leg action, one could strike the ball with wild abandon, but I soon realized there was more to golf than giving the ball a lash.

I was also privileged to caddie for the great Babe Didrickson Zaharias at the old Shaughnessy Heights Golf Course in Vancouver, BC, and learned more about the power generated by a golfer's hip action.

As a fifteen-year-old, I was happy to carry the bag for Ted Kroll, when the tour's leading money winner came to Point Grey for the 1959 BC Open. Out we went to the practice area, and he sent me 150 yards away and hit seven irons at me where I didn't have to take more than a step or two to catch them in my hand on the first bounce and feel the spin sizzle in my palm. I wanted that kind of consistency, but couldn't tell how he did it. All he told me was to "hit it with the same hand position each shot."

Years later, at Capilano for a Seniors Tour Event, I re-introduced myself and reminded Kroll of his victory at Point Grey, and he took the time to show me his interpretation of the impact move he had learned from watching Hogan. Thus another piece was added to the puzzle.

I was also fortunate enough to caddie for legendary entertainer Bing Crosby, and many years later was invited to his famous National Pro-Am at Pebble Beach where I was able to play with, and study, marvelous golfers: Cory Pavin, Hal Sutton, Paul Azinger, Andy Bean, Jim Thorpe, Dick Zokol, Davis Love III, and Jim Furyk. Each one left me with an observation here, or a tip there—certainly no thorough explanation of how they did what they did with a golf ball—but enough perceptions to help develop patterns.

As a senior golfer I was still frustrated to find that I could not call up the repeating swing that produced solid and consistent contact with the ball. With a career, a mortgage, and a family, there was no time to copy a tour player's rigorous practice routine, but I knew that there really must be a secret. Ben Hogan said he had one, but no one could define it. I had a doctorate in historiography, and I was therefore determined to dig it out of the historical maze fashioned from the verbal sharing of tips, weeding out the imagined or the misleading, and tracking down why Ben Hogan was recognized as the greatest ball striker in golf's history—according to no less an appraiser than Jack Nicklaus.

From interviews, watching, and reading, I came to know the parts of what Hogan called his Magical Device, but it was the rare opportunity to play a game with the golfing savant Moe Norman that sparked the "gestalt" as to how it all came together. When Moe's descriptions and observations were confirmed by Stan Leonard, the great Canadian golfer and PGA Tour player, I knew I had the secret, and I proved it to myself by a marked betterment in my play to the point of regularly shooting my age or better. At that point, I believed, it was a good time to pass the secret along.

If you will forgive the meanderings of an aging historiographer, I will put the Hogan story in a context that I hope you find interesting, even if not always on instructional point (which can become a bit tedious anyway). The following photo is a good example of golf's colorful mosaic, whence we are occasionally privileged to enjoy playing this game of ours with some remarkable characters.

Sean Connery is the most avid golfer I know. He has played with royals, celebrities, and hoi polloi—it's the golf that matters to him. Here we arrive by float plane to try a new wilderness course near Campbell River, Vancouver Island.

CHAPTER 1

BEN HOGAN'S BACKGROUND

Many readers will have an expansive knowledge of Ben Hogan's life and struggles. Some younger golfers may not, but if they want to know what determination to win is all about, they should. For champions like Hogan, determination must have a spine of tempered steel and present to us a standard against which we can measure our own level of tenacity. Golf allows others—as well as ourselves—the opportunity to examine character by action, not words. Because of this truth, I will present a brief summary of this remarkable man's singular accomplishments for your consideration.

Ben Hogan was born in the wrong place at the wrong time for any boy to expect a contented and experience-rich childhood; and yet, because of the stress of simply surviving, he most likely gained incredible willpower in the crucible of day-to-day life.

He was born in a cattle town named Stephensville located on the plateau lands of West Texas on August 13, 1912, in a hospital just ten miles away from his family's simple cottage in Dublin. Hot summers and frigid winters were characteristics of this once Comanche country near the Brazos River. It was a time when the Titanic had sunk, and Europe was sliding toward World War I; but, of course, such events were of little concern to the Hogan family. They were worried about the basics, like rent and dinner.

Little Bennie's father was a blacksmith with health problems aggravated by the inexorable change in the territory where a horse culture swept toward a car culture. Bennie and his fourteen-year-old brother, Royal, were in the house when his father and role model chose to shoot himself just above the heart with a thirty-eight caliber pistol. He lingered for twelve hours while newspaper reporters tried to determine which son had witnessed the terrible event, not that it would matter. In a small cottage, anyone at home would have been devastated by the noise of the pistol and horrified by the scene of a bloodied and dying father.

Richard Rhodes, author of *A Hole in the World*, wrote following the suicide of his own mother about "a deep sense of vulnerability ... one parent lost and only one parent left, like one kidney left, or one lung, between me and the void."

Not to put too fine a point on it, but in order to sense the indelible effect his father's suicide left on young Hogan, one should note the impact on Charles Dickens after visiting his father in prison: "No words could express the secret agony in my soul," he wrote.

We can't know how Hogan reacted over time, but can only guess at the nightmarish effect of his loss by contemplating on

how one other quote from Charles Dickens adds an indication of Hogan's burden:

> "My whole nature was so penetrated with the grief and humiliation of such considerations that even now, famous and caressed and happy, I often forget in my dreams that I have a dear wife and children; even that I am a man; and wander desolately back to that time in my life."

Despite the dire contemplations of Dickens, Hogan himself may have made conscious efforts to reconcile the bad hand he had been dealt. Curt Sampson, in his captivating biography titled simply, *Hogan*, quotes the man himself as follows:

> "I feel sorry for rich kids now. I really do. Because they're never going to have the opportunity I had. Because I knew tough things. And I had a tough day all my life and I can handle tough things. They can't. And every day that I progressed was a joy to me, and I recognized it every day. I don't think I could have done what I've done if I hadn't had the tough days to begin with."

Young Hogan's problems did not end with his father's funeral. A determined mother took her brood to Fort Worth to claw out a living. Brother Royal quit school to find work. Bennie helped by selling newspapers at the railroad station and caddying at Glen Garden Drive even though it meant a seven-mile round-trip walk to and from the course. It was said that sometimes he slept on a couple of unsold newspapers in a bunker so that he could be first in line for a bag at sixty-five cents a round.

He met other caddies, including his lifelong friend, Byron Nelson, who was just about the only one who didn't treat this young boy roughly. The caddies had a long driving contest called "Hit for a Chase," in which the caddie who drove range balls the shortest distance had to pick them all up for the others. Bennie fetched a lot of balls. Byron never lost; Bennie never won, and in desperation, even tried hitting cross-handed. At that point Ted Longworth, the club pro, showed Hogan how to move the left hand over the top of the club and the right hand under to get some roll, and young Ben became a long driver of the ball. That caddies' game, in Byron's opinion, drove the small-in-stature Hogan to hook the ball to get that low, hot-running shot that he needed to avoid humiliation. When he turned professional at age seventeen, for the 1920 Texas Open, the hook was the shot that would frustrate his game for many years.

Hogan earned so little money playing the tournament schedule that several times he would have to interrupt his tour for a winner's check and take odd jobs to establish a bankroll that would enable him to get back into the competition he craved. His first pro-golf pay was fifty dollars at Agua Caliente in the Tijuana Open. But, by the time he arrived in Los Angeles, there were just fifteen cents in his pocket, only because he had been living off oranges swiped from inland orchards. His brother Royal loaned him money, as did Ted Leonard, who must have seen the potential in Hogan's determined approach to the game. Seven years after he had "invented" something new to the "Gold Trail"—later to be known as "arduous practice"—Ben

Hogan won his first tournament and $1,100 at the 1938 Four-Ball Invitational in Hershey, Pennsylvania. By 1935 Ben had married Valerie, his best friend and devoted companion for life. She joined him on the tour after their purchase of a secondhand car. Hogan had taken a club job in order to gather the $1,400 needed to finance them out on the road, where it would be slim pickings for the young couple. In *Hogan*, Curt Sampson quotes the reminiscing golfer in a 1983 CBS interview:

"I played the summer tour, and then we started for the winter tour. And we played again in the Pasadena Open, the Los Angeles Open, and I missed the money in the Los Angeles Open. And we were driving to Oakland, California, and Valerie said, 'You know how much money we have?' And I said, 'Yes, I know.' We had eighty-six left out of the $1,400. So she said, 'Well what are we gonna do?' And I said, 'Valerie, we made a deal to spend $1,400. We have $86 left. And we're going to Oakland. So, we shopped all around for a hotel room, the least expensive we could find, and we weren't eating very well and buying no clothes at all.... In the first round of the tournament, I had a fairly early starting time and left the hotel after breakfast and went across the street, and my car was jacked up. And my two rear wheels were sitting on rocks. And they'd even taken the jack. So I came back to the hotel and I bummed a ride with somebody. I can't remember who, now. Anyway. I got to the course and I was late.... So, I played. I won $385. It's the biggest check I'd ever seen in my life."

Ben Hogan's shaky start began the career that would gather honor after honor and one championship after another until the following record would stand as a challenge for all his predecessors.

Ben Hogan's early career tour victories:

1938: Hershey Four-Ball (with Vic Ghezzi).

1940: North and South Open; Greater Greensboro Open; Asheville Open; Hale America Open; Rochester Open.

1941: Asheville Open; Chicago Open; Hershey Open; Miami Biltmore Four-Ball (with Gene Sarazen); Inverness Four-Ball (with Jimmy Demaret).

1942: Los Angeles Open; San Francisco Open; North and South Open; Asheville Open; Hale America Open; Rochester Open.

1945: Nashville Invitational; Portland Open; Richmond Invitational; Montgomery Invitational; Orlando Open.

1946: Phoenix Open; San Antonio Open; St. Petersburg Open; Miami International Four-Ball (with Jimmy Demaret); Colonial Invitational; Western Open; Goodall Round Robin; Inverness Four-Ball (with Jimmy Demaret); Winnipeg Open; PGA Championship; Golden State Open; Dallas Invitational; North and South Open.

1947: Los Angeles Open; Phoenix Open; Colonial National Invitational; Chicago Victory Open (also called the World Championship of Golf); Inverness Four-Ball (with Jimmy Demaret).

1948: Los Angeles Open; PGA Championship; US Open; Inverness Four-Ball (with Jimmy Demaret); Motor City Open; Reading Open; Western Open; Denver Open; Reno Open; Glendale Open.

1949: Bing Crosby Pro-Am; Long Beach Open.

At this point in his career Hogan appeared to have conquered his demons after adjusting his "caddie-swing" grip and polishing his competitive game through the relentless grind of hitting practice balls, forever a favorite pastime. He and his true pal, Valerie, were now in a brand new Cadillac heading to El Paso on a foggy February afternoon.

Ben drove cautiously in the fog, but fate had arranged it so he would meet a ten-ton Greyhound bus just as the twenty-seven-year-old bus driver chose to pass a truck on a narrow bridge at fifty miles per hour.

As depicted in the biopic, *Follow The Sun,* Hogan threw himself across Valerie to protect her. The engine came through the dashboard and smashed his left ankle, crushed his leg, and fractured his pelvis. His left eye was damaged. Doctors told Valerie that he might never walk again, let alone play golf.

Hospitalized for two months, undergoing complex and dangerous surgery, Hogan battled pain, blood clots, and depression, but he hung on. On April 1, 1949, Valerie took Ben home—now weighing only one hundred and twenty pounds—with pain in his left shoulder and leg that he would bear for the rest of his days. Golf was out of the question … or was it?

Seven months after the accident, Hogan went to England as the non-playing captain of the Ryder Cup Team. Upon his return home in September, he began to hit balls again with a stiff-legged swing he developed enough that he decided to try it out at the Los Angeles Open that winter. His weight was up to one hundred and sixty pounds (partially, at least, a result of muscle mass from his rigorous rehabilitation schedule). To everyone's surprise, he tied for first place—in spite of the elastic bandages encasing his legs—only to lose to Sam Snead in a

Monday morning play-off. The good news was that he was back in the game. And besides, that was the lucrative kind of play-off for which players used to pray. For Hogan it was mainly a sign that if he could tolerate the pain, he could compete on a shortened schedule of tournaments.

The 1950 United States Open was held at the Merion Golf Club in Ardmore, Pennsylvania, in June, where Hogan hit a classic one iron to the eighteenth green to set up the win that noted sportswriter Dan Jenkins would call "the most incredible comeback in the history of sports."

Hogan's response was, "It proved that I could still play."

And play he did, as recorded by his championships that followed:

1950: U.S. Open.

1951: The Masters; U.S. Open; World Championship of Golf.

1952: Colonial National Invitational.

1953: The Masters; Pan American Open; Colonial National Invitational; U.S. Open; The Open Championship (at Carnoustie).

1959: Colonial National Invitational.

The claustrophobic sixth hole at Carnoustie was 565 yards long, with bunkers that could house a Volkswagen. They were placed near the landing area to catch any misaligned drives, with another set of bunkers waiting for the second shot as well. While most players, like former Open champion Bob Locke, hit four iron, seven iron to lay up, Ben Hogan hit full driver down a narrow strip of brown grass running between out-of-bounds on the left and the fairway to the right, which was pockmarked with bunkers. He ignored the main fairway altogether, then hit

his spoon to the green over more traps and a twisting burn. This he did each day with birdies each round. Members of Carnoustie who came to love the "Wee Ice Mon," refer to this pathway as "Hogan's Alley."

Now that you have some background ... shall we begin?

(AP/WideWorld)

Ben Hogan drives at the sixth hole at Carnoustie, 1953. Caddie Cecil Timms almost drove the Hawk crazy with constant smiles and chatter. Worse, he would cover his eyes when Hogan putted. Hogan, however, was in complete control as one can see by his hands still grasping the club with his characteristic moulded grip. Hogan was heard to say, "Timmy, shut your mouth and stand still."

CHAPTER 2

INTRODUCTION TO THE SECRET

B en Hogan was the greatest ball-striker in the history of golf according to his peers, and most of those who study the game will agree. No less an observer than Jack Nicklaus stated:

"So many things about Hogan were special. He was the greatest shot-maker I ever saw. He was more determined and could totally out-focus anyone else in his time of playing. No one seemed to know him very well, which made him that much more feared as a competitor. He probably worked harder than anyone to reach the top, and it took him a long time. Then, when he got there, his body was all but destroyed by the car accident. All he

did was start all over again at nearly forty, and got even better. Nobody was like Hogan."

It was believed that Hogan had a secret because he hit the ball so purely, so consistently. He attempted to explain his trial-and-error discovery in *Life* magazine's August 8, 1955 issue, but there were errors in the misuse of anatomical terms, exemplified by the following vague statements, devoid of defined terms and clarity:

"I cupped the wrist gradually backward and inward on the back-swing so that the wrist formed a slight V at the top of the swing. The angle was not more than four or six degrees, almost invisible to the human eye. This simple maneuver, in addition to prona-tion, had the effect of opening the face of the club to the widest practical extreme at the top of the swing."

Hogan acknowledged the confusion in the article when he stated, "I doubt if it will be worth a doggone [thing] to the weekend duffer, and it might ruin a bad golfer."

Mr. Hogan planned to clarify the misleading information and the several tantalizing hints he left behind. Unfortunately, before he could be persuaded to properly describe the Magical Device and how to apply it, he passed away. In the decades that followed, so many different opinions were advanced among top professionals as to have rendered them all useless. Here are some, as listed in the March 1994 issue of *Golf Digest,* as well as some more recent sources:

- Ken Venturi: "It was psychological."
- Cary Middlecoff: "It was the way he stuck his right elbow into his stomach."
- Jack Burke, Jr.: "It was the way he used his right hand."
- Dick Harmon: "It was his strong lateral move on the downswing."
- Gardner Dickinson: "It was his ball and hand position."
- Bob Toski: "He stabilized the force of the blow with his left arm and hand."
- Johnny Miller: "It was the way he buckled his left wrist."
- Byron Nelson: "It was his left-hand grip."
- Chuck Cook: "It was the stiffer shafts in his clubs."
- Jody Vasquez: "The secret is the correct functioning of the right leg."
- T. J. Tomasi: "The cupped left wrist opens the club face."
- Gene Sarazen: "He has it up here" (pointing to his head).
- Jimmy Demaret: "I think the key to Hogan's swing was the ready position—when he dropped his hands into the 'slot.' I believe this was the real secret."
- Tom Bertrand: "The left elbow turns inward to square up the face of the club."

In spite of the incredible interest in the secret, nobody has been able to describe—with properly defined anatomical terms—just

(Courtesy of Arv Olson and Linda Leonard)

Sam Snead, Stan Leonard, Fred Wood, and Ben Hogan eating lunch in the men's locker room at old Shaughnessy Heights Golf Course, Vancouver, 1945.

how to apply the technique within the structure Hogan called his Magical Device. And certainly amateurs, however talented they may be, rarely have the time to "dig it out of the dirt" as Hogan did. If they knew the secret, perhaps they could shorten the time required to maintain high standards in this complex game we call golf. With great humility, I intend to try.

The touring players pictured above were photographed in the locker room because professional athletes of the day were not permitted in the clubhouse with amateurs who supposedly played only for the "love" of the game. And so, it was a glass of milk and an egg sandwich before their exhibition round. Of course, they would readily acknowledge that Walter Hagen had gotten them at least that far by changing into his spiked shoes before exhibitions in a chauffeured limousine parked close by the first tee. He would keep the window curtains drawn until emerging dramatically to an applauding crowd. All this was to point out that the pros of his day were not even allowed into the dressing room.

Of course, we must remember that this unctuous atmosphere was not because golf was the pastime of only the idle rich as the Hollywood cliché presented; there are at least two important factors defining "socio-economic" status: wealth *and* education. Robert Trent Jones and Sir Michael Bonallack had the advantage of extensive schooling. Ben Hogan and Sir Sean Connery did not. Hogan, for all intents and purposes, left the classroom long before officially dropping out of high school. Connery quit at twelve. Both left for the same fundamental reason of helping to put "bread on the table." What makes them both so remarkable is that we now review their records of how they developed their "art forms" to extraordinary levels, and can reflect on the great human qualities of desire and tenacity which not only helps define genius, but also challenges the rest of us to a little more effort with our own projects.

I have interviewed Ben Hogan's fellow competitors, such as Sam Snead, Stan Leonard, Ted Kroll, Mike Souchak, Fred Woods, George Knudson, Jack Nicklaus, Moe Norman, Alvie Thompson, and Ernie Brown. I have interviewed caddies and ball shaggers the great man employed, and I have read most of what has been written about him. I even had the thrill of once watching him hit balls at old Shaughnessy in Vancouver.

Furthermore, I have had the rare privilege of caddying for, and playing with, Moe Norman, the golfing savant who worshipped Hogan. "He stood there and watched me hit balls— Mr. Hogan watched me!" Moe stated proudly in a rare unguarded moment. "He knows the secret, and I know the secret.

We both do it." In his unique way, Norman showed me the hand action he believed Mr. Hogan used to hit shot after shot with such impact and consistency. I was fascinated, but a bit leery. However, when I had finally sifted through all the theories, the extrapolation of facts, and the hypotheses, the pieces of the puzzle finally came together. Excited, but still unsure, I joined Stan Leonard, the great Canadian PGA tour player, on his daily walk up Forty-ninth Avenue, which cuts through a quiet, well gardened residential area of Vancouver. Stan the Man was so like Hogan—he had the same intimidating affect and did not "suffer fools gladly." Leonard had phoned me about a magazine article I had written, complimenting my appraisal of the last Canadian Open tournament and how the modern professionals seemed to have forgotten the struggle by the older generation of touring professionals like Hagen, Sarazen, Hogan, Snead, and Palmer, who had worked so hard to make golf popular. The article mentioned the fact that Vijay Singh had been flown to the Canadian Open at the New Shaughnessy Golf and Country Club in Vancouver, and that he had been given free hotel services as well as a prestige courtesy car. At the media session, Vijay admitted, "We tour in luxury, and we're really spoiled." With all this posh treatment, I found it jarring to hear that Vijay called a Black Top cab at the Bayshore Hotel near Stanley Park that night and asked the driver, Pat James, if he knew of a good French restaurant. The answer was, "Yes, Sir," and Pat drove him into town where the fare came to $4.70. Vijay handed Pat a five-dollar bill with a keep-the-change wave of the hand. The cabbie looked at the thirty-cent windfall, not knowing what to say, but diplomatically suggested, "Well, would you at least autograph it?" And with an embarrassed smile Vijay did. But I remembered Lee Trevino, who would carry around a roll of twenties for situations like that, and had left a generous trail behind him wherever he went. Stan Leonard agreed because he remembered when thirty cents was about all golfers like Hogan had.

As we discussed the ins and outs of golf, I got up enough nerve to ask Stan about Hogan's swing. Stan stopped to stare at me with those searching eyes. I thought he would walk away. He was nearing ninety years of age and didn't have time for idle chitchat (just as Hogan never did) but to my surprise, he opened up.

"Do you remember the bunker lesson I gave you a couple of years ago?"

"Of course I do."

"Well," Stan divulged slowly, "I didn't tell you everything."

I wasn't surprised, because Stan had often remarked that Ben Hogan had taught him one lesson, with bone-jarring bluntness—"Never give secrets away free. They're yours. Make them pay for it."

Stan stepped under the shade of a boulevard tree out of the hot sun, and told me where I was correct in my analysis, and where it could use a little polish here and there. Then he gave me his personal insight

Cabbie Pat James with Vijay's autograph.

and interpretation on the Hogan theme. What he also did was to corroborate Moe Norman's analysis (which, as you will find later, was similar in hand action, although his setup was replete with idiosyncrasies). The results were the same, however, as the ball was crushed on the sweet spot time after time after time.

After our walk, I left Stan more excited than ever and hurried down southwest Marine Drive to Point Grey Golf Club's practice fairway to begin using the Magical Device and the secret move hidden carefully within it.

Two weeks later I shot a sixty-nine, three strokes under par at the public university course, and two strokes under my age. It was then that I began to shoot my age or better regularly, at least when my putter cooperated. More significantly, I shot my age or better nine times during competition, which might make you think that the system laid out in the pages that follow is definitely worth a close study.

CHAPTER 3

THE GENERAL PROBLEM

How can an amateur golfer strike the ball consistently well without daily play and without hitting thousands of practice balls each week?

Have you ever found that no matter how many lessons you take or how much you train, there is the nagging feeling that the pros are holding back some valuable information? Then, out of nowhere, you encounter brief golfing moments when you'd like to live forever. Forces of the universe pause during their mysterious work among the galaxies for just long enough to allow you to somehow guide the sweet spot of your club face through that infinitesimal center of gravity at the heart of your golf ball. The results are addictive, and like the cocaine habitué, we spend a large part of our golf season casting about, waiting for the next soul-satisfying thrill. Surely, the gods toy with us, because that elusive pure hit, once achieved, must be nothing more than an accident of physics, a random journey through the geometric, jumbled confusion of angles and arcs, levers and planes, to make a repeat of that pure stroke doubtful, if not impossible. We are, after all, wandering the unknown and unseen dimensions of applied physics, hoping for duplication—like the proverbial ten million chimpanzees hammering at ten million typewriters hoping for one Shakespearean sonnet. We realize with despair that we seek perfection. Impossible, and yet …

Some golfers seem to achieve more of these pure hits than others. They write lengthy, tortuous books on the subject— books that would cross a physicist's eyes. Such tomes need an engineer's dictionary for reference, and have been held up as the major factor responsible for destroying the careers of at least two professional tour players, leaving the once successful competitor talking to himself about lost or stressed levers when he, before all others, would admit that his mind should be absorbed with the image of his target and not the mechanics of his swing.

There are examples of golfers who have quit this fruitless quest, realizing after time that we are chasing perfection after all, and in the end, most of us find that we can not attain it for more than brief flashes. Mike Souchak acknowledged at Capilano on the Senior Tour in 1981 that the gods had smiled on him during the 1955 Texas Open, when he shot rounds that still stood as PGA competitive records: 27 strokes for nine holes; 60 for eighteen; and 257 for seventy-two. "I had one three-putt green for my sixty," Souchak mentioned. "Other than that, things went well."

Tiger Woods might win a tournament coming from behind by remarkably holing six straight birdies, yet even the game's greatest golfer cannot achieve perfection. The chaotic and butchered passes at the ball that Tiger knew all too much about, but which had somehow escaped our scrutiny, offer an explanation that makes us wonder if Tiger really did win. Perfection is so hard to find.

CHAPTER 4

THE CONTEXT: HOGAN'S FUNDAMENTALS REVIEWED

When I first described the Magical Device, I assumed that everyone would be clearly aware of Mr. Hogan's elaborate preparatory moves to position himself properly before beginning his precise and distinct swing. However, like most "assumptions," I was, no doubt, wrong.

Those who have read Hogan's *Five Lessons* devoured the details, and shared them in long and focused discussions with friends on the wealth of insights Hogan presented in his deliberate and detailed way.

Sidney L. James, the former managing editor of *Sports Illustrated,* wrote:

"It has been *Sports Illustrated*'s privilege to bring this master's fundamental wisdom to a wide audience by teaming him with the No.1 writer of the nation, Herbert Warren Wind, and an artist with a special gift for freezing action into vivid instructional pictures, Anthony Ravielli. This team—Hogan, Wind, Ravielli—has produced what I believe to be a classic of golf instruction. It cannot fail to improve the game of anyone who puts it to work for him. That is not my opinion alone. Thousands of golfers who have read the text and studied the illustrations during the serialization in *Sports Illustrated* have mailed in delighted (and unsolicited) testimonials. The Hogan-Wind-Ravielli prescription works. It even worked for me, a humbled and hopeful editor."

But that was then; and this is now.

It is impossible to know how widespread familiarity with Ben Hogan's setup is in the twenty-first century, so I propose a brief review that one should consider before attempting to employ the Magical Device.

If you are a student of Hogan's pre-swing methods and understand (or utilize) his advice on the grip or setup, you can move ahead to the section on the Magical Device. If not, let me quickly summarize what Ben Hogan believed to be the basic fundamentals of a sound golf swing. Whether you use some of them or none of them is up to you, but chances are you should be in tune with them, and at least understand why you are not using this

item or that. But Hogan believed that "the average golfer is entirely capable of building a repeating swing and breaking eighty, if he learns to perform a small number of correct movements and conversely, it follows, eliminates a lot of movements which tend to keep the swing from repeating."

If this is not your problem or way to improve, sweep by to chapter 5.

Grip

Hogan was very precise about his grip. It began with a "long left thumb" when he was to call on his power fade.

Hogan held the club in the palm of his left hand running from the pad at the base of the palm to the pad at the base of his forefinger.

The last three fingers squeeze stability into the left hand structure. Snead said that he "wanted to squeeze the juice out of it."

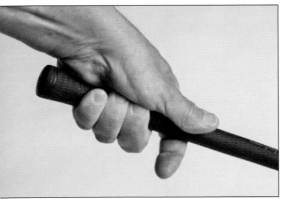

Hogan didn't argue.

"You have to hold on to the club for a hard hit don't you?" he answered when asked about the importance of a firm and proper grip.

The forearms stay comfortable so that stiffness does not impair rhythm. There is a familiar strength in the hands, which allow shoulders and arms to be held in a relaxed anticipation of coming effort—but the strength is there.

The little finger of the right hand fits around the groove offered by the forefinger and middle finger of the left hand. The two central fingers of the right hand close the left thumb snugly into the palm of the right hand. The thumb and forefinger of the right hand fit high on top, in a softer grasp. A squeeze of the controlling last three fingers of the left hand and the last two fingers of the right hand unites the hands into a strong unit.

Completed grip.

Stance

Hogan's stance reflected his pursuit of a steady foundation for his swing. The right foot was square to the target line. For full shots with long-shafted clubs, the left foot angled toward the target from a "closed" position. The right knee was rock-steady in its place with the weight on the inside edge of the foot—and never on the outside edge or the little toe. The same inside edge pressure was needed for the left foot, where the weight was focused on the big toe.

The right elbow rests on the crest of the pelvis ready to act a fulcrum. The shoulders are square to the target line, and the armpits are connected to the rib cage.

Hogan used a wide stance for the driver but adjusted his stance according to the length of the shaft and the distance required for the shot. The ball was aligned off the left heel for consistent trajectory, and the right foot came closer to the target line if he were using a short shafted club.

(Courtesy of Mike Lilly)

Here is another solid-looking stance by Tiger Woods, the man chasing Ben Hogan's records. Note the hovering club head for an unrestricted take-away.

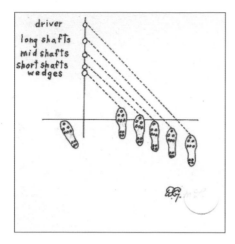

Half-way down to impact zone back to target.

At the top of the backswing, the right elbow has been pulled away from the right hip. The right knee has not moved from its flexed position, pointing at a perpendicular angle to the target line.

Plane

Envisioning Hogan's swing plane is a bit tricky if you have not yet seen Ravielli's inventive drawing in which Hogan imagines his head poking out through a hole in a pane of glass angling down squarely to the target line. We shall see this later, but to continue talking about the swing plane for just another moment, many of you will know that Hogan changed the square glass image as he came down into the ball by turning his back on the target and raising his left shoulder to bring down the hands. The shoulders changed from their parallel position to the target line, and turned into a slightly "closed" position. (We get to plane in detail in chapter 15.)

In preparation for coming down into the impact zone, the left knee has moved over to the left foot and is flexed as well. The right knee has remained still and stable to this point.

Swing to the top: full shot

The move to the top is initiated by a tilt of the shoulders with the rest of the body remaining still. The effect is that the back of the left hand looks down at the ground with the right palm also facing the ground. This position changes as the hands approach the outside of the right hip. Here the shoulders are pulled into their turn to the top, and the hands change with the cocking of both wrists.

Once the hands reach the waist, the left shoulder rises and the left hip clears the way for the right knee to turn quickly through the ball.

At impact, the head remains behind the ball and the center of the chest and the belt buckle begin their turn toward the target. Both knees remain flexed throughout the swing.

Swing to the finish

Now let's look at the engine room of the swing in detail and how Hogan used his hands.

The swing to the finish reflects the steady balance shown throughout the swing from the address to the top of the backswing, through impact, and then to the follow-through.

At this highest point of the follow-through, the golfer should be comfortable up on "the dirty toe" of the right foot, which demonstrates the complete release of the right side through the ball. (More on this coming up.) The belt buckle faces the target.

Once again, the completed swing should reflect the balance Hogan strived for on every shot. The old pros used to say, "Pose for the photograph—two seconds."

CHAPTER 5

DEFINING APPLICABLE TERMS AND THEIR PROPER USE

Before any serious discussion can begin on any topic, one must always define and agree on the use of terminology so that communication has at least a chance of clarity. Mr. Hogan knew, with great confidence, what he was doing and how he was swinging the club so repetitively into the ball. But how can we communicate these thoughts and feelings repeated so often in hours of practice in an era where a couple of putts and shoulder stretches seemed to do the trick for everyone else but Hogan?

It is becoming apparent to more and more golf analysts that Mr. Hogan did not use universally accepted definitions for some of his physical actions, and that was the problem for many who discovered new ways to snap-hook or shank the ball.

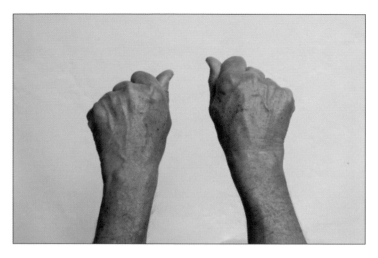

Pronation. From a "palms up" position, rotating the hands and forearms inward to face down.

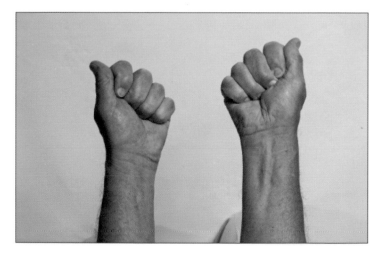

Supination. From a "palms down" position, rotating the hands and forearms outward to face up.

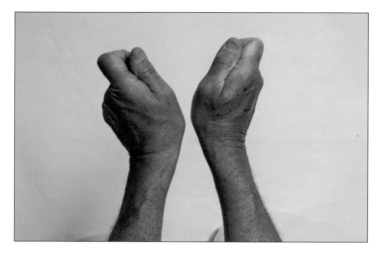

Dorsi-flexion. Raising the top of the hand alone as if to touch knuckles to the wrist and producing a concave or cupped wrist.

Palmar-flexion. Curling the palm into itself as if to make a fist and producing a convex or bowed wrist—with an arch.

Here are some basic terms we shall use in describing the Magical Device and the secret within.

Pronation and supination

Mr. Hogan spoke about pronation on the backswing, and then after the downswing, supination on the forward swing into the ball, but there is no clear direction as to how to do that. Which hand was he talking about? At what stage do you pronate or supinate? With the whole arm? Besides, this was not the action within the Magical Device. In fact, it is precisely with these issues that the confusion surrounding the secret lies.

It should be noted that a golfer can supinate or pronate only one hand at a time. The unwary player would pronate his left hand on the take-away, which would open the blade ("lay the club off") with the risk of getting the club "stuck behind" him at the top. In a desperate attempt to square the club at impact, the golfer might pronate the right hand without the hope of getting things back to "square" with any regularity. Tiger Woods calls this action "flipping the wrists" and warns young golfers who use it in their attempt to get extra distance that they are heading for control problems with devastating results at times. Besides, Hogan did not flip or pronate, as you shall see.

The Magical Device: What controlled Hogan's swing in the impact zone?

Let's examine what Hogan did in the engine room of his swing, so that we can understand the structure and the mechanics of what he called his Magical Device, and, after that, how to apply the secret move within this structure.

Ben Hogan was precise to the extreme about how he set up for the swing. His description of the grip, stance, and plane

of his swing are well presented in *Five Lessons*. But you can re-examine these important points in terms of your own physique and level of experience. It is my belief that a great many golfers with sound swings, with characteristics that differ from Hogan's, would greatly benefit from learning just the mechanics of the Magical Device and of the application of the secret in particular.

These two structural improvements will deliver a solid consistency to striking the ball no matter how idiosyncratic your swing may be. So, for now, we shall look at the construction of his Magical Device, which is really the special relationship of his arms, hands, and shoulders—a supported triangle which moves as a unit.

The Magical Device. Notice that the inside dimples of the elbows point skyward, thus preventing further supination of the left arm or pronation of the right arm.

Hogan emphasized the position of the arms, which are "connected" to the rib cage by the pressure of the inside of the left bicep to the left pectoral muscle and the right bicep touching the right side of the rib cage (like Vijay Singh, with his glove tucked under his armpit at practice for staying "connected"). The special focus here is how close the elbows are to each other,

This triangle is the Magical Device that supported Ben Hogan's power fade. Notice the connection by the inside of the upper arms to the rib cage. With this connection, the arms and hands do not swing independently within this structurally strong unit. They are turned through impact by the forceful rotation of Hogan's torso, and pushed by his driving right side.

(Photo by Jules Alexander)

and the fact that the "dimples" on the insides of both elbows are pointing to the sky. The right elbow is touching the crest of the right hip and is a valuable contact point. This triangle, composed of hands, arms, and shoulders, is what Hogan called his Magical Device, and he moved it as a unit, in the powerful way shown earlier.

We shall get into the full shot later, in more detail, step by step. For now, just to get used to the Magical Device, you should try it out with short putts.

CHAPTER 6

HOGAN'S MAGICAL DEVICE: TRY IT PUTTING

S tan Leonard was, at one time, Canada's most successful golfer, after leaving his Head Pro job at Marine Drive Golf Club in Vancouver at the ripened age of forty to try his hand in the PGA Tour.

Hogan was Stan's model, and he studied this man who was so close to his own size and demeanor. He dressed like Hogan and acted like him. There was no reason why he couldn't play like the steely-eyed champion they called the Hawk, and he was not surprised when he won three PGA titles: the Greater Greensboro Open in 1957, the Las Vegas Tournament of Champions in 1958, and the Western Open in 1960. The Las Vegas tournament became the most lucrative title of Stan's career when, at a time when most winners' checks were around $2,000, 10,000 silver dollars were brought to him in a wheelbarrow after four rounds of sound ball striking and controlled putting.

Later that evening, Stan received a phone call from a guest in the hotel's penthouse inviting him up for a drink. "I have a present for you," the friendly voice added. Stan was understandably curious and very surprised when the grateful bettor handed him another check matching his first prize winnings. "I can't take this," Stan said apprehensively, looking at five years worth of salary for a school teacher in 1958.

Packing to leave for the "big show."

"Well I insist," the pleasant stranger joked, "because I won a lot more than that by backing your skills today—and I'm happy to give you ten percent."

Stan looked at the man carefully and shrugged.

"I suppose you're wondering if that check's any good," the man laughed, "so hurry downstairs and cash it. Then come on back up for that drink."

That is how Stan Leonard earned $20,000 for winning a tournament at a time when one could buy a very large house with that kind of money. He and the stranger, Gordon McRae—star of the musical *Oklahoma*—became fast friends.

More than that, Stan had won everything there was to win on the Canadian Tour many times over and, as a result of his CPGA titles, had earned invitations to nine of Augusta's Masters tournaments. In this prestigious event, Stan had established a most enviable record and was just a putt or two away from wins in 1958, 1959, and 1960. Of course, Stan could sink a putt when he had to, and playing informally one special summer twilight at Point Grey in Vancouver, he told me why.

(Courtesy of Linda Leonard)

Striking the ball using the Magical Device.

The hands do not move in isolation. The Magical Device moves them on plane and on path while the right elbow acts like a fulcrum against the crest of the right hip. The lower body is still. Arnold Palmer kept his body still by pressing his knees inward; Stan Leonard pressed his knees outward for the same important effect.

"Take Hogan's address position with arched wrists and a firm squeeze of the middle fingers to make the hands into a solid unit," he said. "Hold it through impact and you have one hell of a chance of nailing six footers. That's the way he did it before his left eye was damaged. For short putts you first tilt the triangle with a push down from the left shoulder. Then pull the shoulder back up, and the club head moves through the ball with the left hand dominating. For long putts, use the right hand and right shoulder to push the left shoulder back up and through the ball. The sensitivity of the right hand helps gauge distance. The triangle gives you reliability for distance if you connect to the large muscles involved in the stroke."

According to Leonard, Hogan wanted to control the putter with his arms and shoulders—that is to say, with the connected body parts he dubbed the Magical Device. By moving the triangle made by the hands, arms, and shoulders, he could develop consistency when delivering the club head to the ball, as well as administer a better roll by striking the ball on the upswing. Ben Crenshaw, widely acknowledged as one of the best putters on tour, and as one of the foremost golf-history buffs in the game, spoke fondly of Hogan's putting stroke. He was on the plane from Monterey to San Francisco advising ardent listener, Andy Williams of Moon River fame, to raise his left shoulder to roll the ball into the cup.

Palmar flexion: using Hogan's grip for putting

The centerpiece to the Magical Device is the left hand, which is held in a subtle but vital position not readily observable. This move involves flexing the left palm by squeezing the last three

fingers as you arch the left wrist into a convex position with a bulge toward the target. It is like making a fist with a strong flat wrist without a trace of a concave or collapsed angle. This movement is called "palmar-flexion." Breaking down the left wrist is, of course, an amateur's biggest weakness.

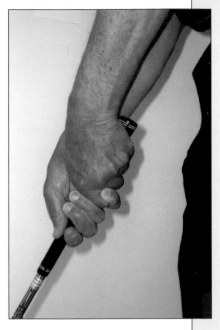

With the left hand in the proper position, take note of the strong position of both hands ready with the structural strength required for solid impact. Here we can see (1) the arch of the left wrist, and (2) the left wrist bulging toward the target by the squeeze and twist of the last three fingers into the left palm.

When putting, arch the wrists by pressing the putter head into the ground with both thumbs pointing down the shaft. Raise the shoulders until the head of the putter is off the ground slightly, and keep it hovering to reduce grip tension and overuse of the hands. The ball position is forward, so that both thumbs point to the ball. (Personal preferences will develop with practice.)

When ready to strike the ball, the left shoulder pushes down and tilts the triangle of shoulders, hands, and arms away from the ball and back down the imagined target line. The right hand is in a firm dorsi-flexed position and is held in that solid arched position throughout the stroke as the left shoulder moves toward the chin on the takeaway. The back of the left hand angles down to ground and to the back of the ball. The Magical Device moves the hands.

At impact, the lower body foundation is quiet. Knees are flexed in the "sitting on the bar-stool" position. The Magical Device tilts as a separate unit when the left shoulder is raised. Left shoulder up— ball in the cup.

As the left shoulder pulls "up" on the through-swing, the right shoulder moves toward the chin on the inside path set by the left shoulder parallel to the target line (not "over the top" of it). The left forearm does not "over-rotate" in supination if the left elbow dimple is pointed to the sky, as Hogan recommended. With this elbow position the ball rolls to where the putter is aimed.

The hands never change grip position, so when the hands pass through the ball with the dimple of the left elbow facing out toward the ball and the target line,

the hands stay in the position assumed at address and move in unison with the tilting shoulders. The back of the left hand is arched by the thumb pressing down hard and looking "down the line" toward the cup.

Some details to emphasize

1. You will notice that when you tilt the Magical Device without changing the triangle, or your grip, that the back of the left hand looks to the ground behind the ball as the left shoulder pushes down to begin the take-away.

2. Don't move the hands. Let the Magical Device move them. And get used to hovering the club head at address. It helps everything stay firm but relaxed. (It worked for Jack Nicklaus.)

(Courtesy of Nicklaus North Golf Club)

3. After you strike the ball, the hands continue down the line, holding the same position with no change in the wrist arch or the right hand's dorsi-flexion, and you are effortlessly and confidently hitting through the ball with no deceleration.

4. You will also notice that there has been no "hit and stop," which is a "block" to the release of the right side, as the chest's center moves through the ball.

5. More than that, you will see that there is absolutely no breakdown of the left wrist as the club head goes down the line.

6. The knees remain quiet and flexed in the "sit down" position. There is no head movement or movement below the waist during the backswing. And certainly no straightening of the left leg at all.

7. To add to the "resistance-free" pull of the left shoulder through impact (left shoulder up—ball in the cup), the right elbow, which has been "connected" to the right hip area, is easily pulled toward the belt buckle to follow the club head on the follow-through. The effect is the easy feeling of a solid hit through the ball, with impressive accuracy.

Drill: try three- to six-footers every day for a week

Before you try to put this into your game, give it a week of practice with about forty balls a day. Find a piece of carpet in the basement. Get used to the fluid and relaxed strokes when the club head is not grounded. Just tilt the Magical Device for seven days in a row, anywhere you can get it done.

(Courtesy of Ross Collver)

Hogan putting in Jasper, 1953. Note the ball in line with the left toe. Thumbs point toward the ball. Putter is hovering. This baby's in.

A brief pause

There are at least a couple of ways you can go about this:

1. You can try it for five minutes and go back, in disgust, to your old style.

2.   You could persevere with forty practice balls a day for one week. Find a strip of carpet and try it. Use different putters if you like, just to see if you can sink ten six-footers in row with each of them, and discover that it ain't the arrow, it's the Indian.

This putting drill is just a way to introduce you to a system step by step, rather than burying you with a great many details at once. If you get bored, you can move on to apply this putting stroke to short chips. Ingrain the feel of strong hands by powering and stabilizing the stroke with the Magical Device, and get ready to move on through longer chips, to lobs, and half-shots.

CHAPTER 7

THE NEXT STEP: CHIPPING WITH THE MAGICAL DEVICE

Ernie Brown, the affable pro who was Head Professional at Vancouver's Quilchena Golf Club for so many years, remembers Hogan from 1947, when the PGA Tour was still struggling to recover from World War II. Ernie drove to Los Angeles from Vancouver to pick up the tour and try his luck on the "Gold Trail." It was here he first met Ben Hogan, who arrived from Texas by train, and Ernie offered Ben a ride to Portland, the next tour stop. After winning in Oregon, the usually taciturn Ben Hogan became more friendly as they drove up the Pacific Coast to Seattle, and by the time they reached their third stop in Vancouver, Hogan was even more relaxed, so much so that he asked Ernie, "How 'bout fixing that grip of yours a bit?

Get that left thumb down the shaft a little. Arch both the hands when you chip."

He then suggested that Ernie try the method of chipping described below, which is only a small step away from the putting stroke and a good way to become more familiar with the Magical Device.

Take your six iron. Chip a few balls ten to twenty feet with the hands held firmly in an arched position, thumbs pointing down at the ball. Now, with just a small push down by the left shoulder, the club head moves back as the triangle tilts. It is held in line because the point of the right elbow is connected to a stable right hip—to act as a fulcrum as when putting.

Now, a short raising of the left shoulder tilts the triangle, and the club chips the ball onto the green. Here is another extremely effective nuance of Hogan's Magical Device for chipping. The elbow dimples are pointing upward toward the sky, and the impact position is assumed at address—open stance, weight shifted left, and with just a short take-away that is controlled by the left

shoulder. The impact position for the hands is maintained throughout the chip, which has the effect of the back of the left hand facing down at the back of the ball—just like a long putt.

As the short chips become longer into lobs and three-quarter swing shots, the lower body is brought into play in a special way, as we shall soon see. But while chipping, you bring the Magical Device back through the ball by raising the left shoulder. This gives you a solid feel because of the arched hand position, and the stability provided by the torso connected to the arms by pressure at the armpits, as well as the right elbow attached to the crest of the hip.

Don't let the hands move independently. The Magical Device moves them through the ball. Put together with a steady, flexed right knee, and a right elbow that returns to the hip as the Magical Device enters the impact zone, there is impressive strength and improved swing repetition as you advance from chipping to lobs to three-quarter shots with good solid contact.

If the chipping action is not readily absorbed, don't panic. Keep putting

(Courtesy of Doug Brown)

Ernie Brown holds his balance and grip for longer shots.

and keep chipping this way a few more sessions until the action feels natural.

In his books, Hogan encouraged golfers to "practice his drills fifteen minutes per day for one week." This prescription is surprisingly close to laboratory research, which states, "For an action to be absorbed into a reflex response, the action should be repeated fifty times per day in conscious repetition—for seven days." By then, it should have been programmed into the left side of your brain.

When the chipping action has been absorbed, it's time to try the same action for lobs and three-quarter shots.

Stan Leonard uses the Magical Device to launch a strong half-shot.

(Courtesy of Linda Leonard)

CHAPTER 8

THE SECRET MOVE WITHIN THE MAGICAL DEVICE

Now for Hogan's secret, which was essentially the manner in which he moved his hands within the Magical Device. He has left many a false trail, perhaps for fun, maybe just because an interviewer annoyed him. Ben Hogan did not suffer fools gladly. He had his reasons for low levels of trust.

Three key questions for applying the secret

1. How did Mr. Hogan get both hands from the dorsi-flexed (concave) position at the top of his backswing to their proper positions at impact?

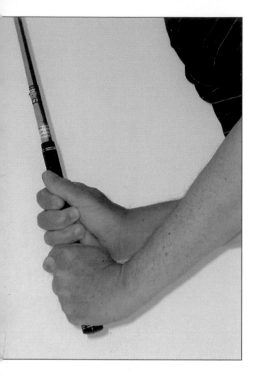

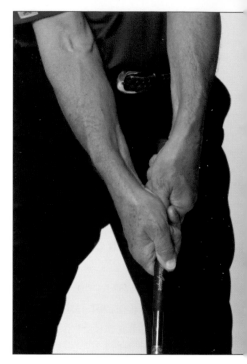

2. What are the two distinct features for the left hand at impact? It is arched, with a convex bulge toward the target.
3. What is the role of the right hand? It remains concave in dorsi-flexion throughout the impact zone.

The answers to these three questions help describe how

Mr. Hogan applied the structurally powerful secret within the Magical Device. Both hands hold their dorsi-flexion from the top down to the impact zone.

What exactly did Hogan do just before impact?

At the top of his backswing, he had both left and right wrists in the concave position of dorsi-flexion. This was achieved largely by the "cocking" of the wrists as they pass the waist on the way to the horizonal position. Some old pros talked about "holding a tray with the right hand," like a waiter, if they went to extremes with the dorsi-flexion of the right hand at the top of the backswing. Whatever one calls that concave hand position, it is designed to open the club face, and it sets up the secret that Hogan applied just before impact.

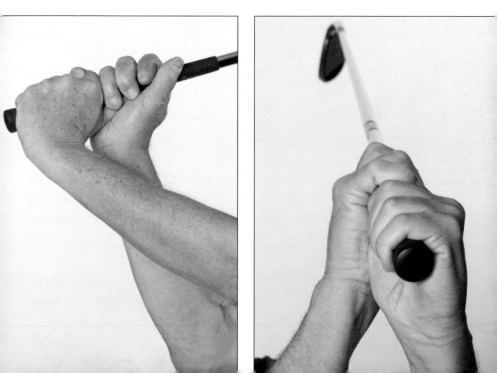

Coming down to the impact zone

Just before the hands reach the top of the backswing, the knees begin to move into a semi-sitting position. At this point the left shoulder is at its lowest, and the first upward movement of the left shoulder tilts the Magical Device. The hands drop into a position called the "slot" on their way to the impact zone. The right elbow reconnects to the right hip, and the Magical Device is ready to absorb the power of the torso (a key move to be discussed later). The hands hold their dorsi-flexion. The elbow dimple points to the sky and the secret is ready to be applied.

On top of a rock solid foundation, Ben Hogan is about to apply the secret within his Magical Device.

(Courtesy of Jules Alexander)

CHAPTER 9

HAND ACTION THROUGH THE IMPACT ZONE

Here is an artist's interpretation of the left hand through impact. Bear in mind that the hand is not "flipping" over—it is being turned through the ball by rotating the torso as the left hand twists and arches. The left arm is held in one position where the inside dimple looks up to the sky—there is no rolling of either arm.

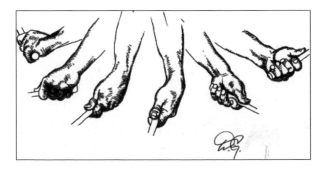

Twist and arch

The golfer squeezes the last three fingers of the left hand as he arches his hand. The left thumb points to the ball and now the secret is applied as palmar-flexion brings an arched and convex wrist into the ball.

Here is the way Hogan set up his left hand for the stress of impact. Golfing savant and lifelong Hogan-watcher Moe Norman puts the secret to the

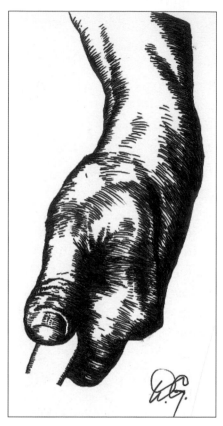

(Courtesy of Todd Graves)

test. The right hand holds its concave set. The left hand is arched and bulges in a convex position toward the target

Keen-eyed television broadcaster and 1973 U.S. Open champion, Johnny Miller, made a telling observation one day years ago. He thought that Hogan "buckled" his left wrist into the ball and no doubt could have demonstrated the action, although it was difficult at that time to decide what he meant by this term.

I was determined to ask him while at the Bing Crosby National Pro-Am but could not seem to bump into him during a quiet moment, as these tour players have a stress-filled daily schedule and are constantly approached by fans with dumb questions to ask. To make matters worse—actually impossible—Miller tied for first place in the Sunday round with the pre-eminent Jack Nicklaus, and I was never able to ask him about what he meant by "buckle."

As luck would have it, though, I successfully tracked down Jean-Paul Hebert, son of Jay Hebert, the PGA professional golfer and friend of Ben Hogan. I had shagged for Jay and had followed him, and his brother Lionel, when they played the BC Centennial Open at Point Grey in 1958. I wanted to know more about Hogan. Jay was younger than Hogan, but became accepted company as the Hawk grew more mellow with success.

Jay had fought as a captain in the Marines in World War II and had taken up photography while recovering from leg wounds received in the battle of Iwo Jima. When Hogan came to a golf clinic at Moon Brook Country Club in Jamestown, New York, Jay asked Hogan if he "could take a couple of pictures." Without the luxury of modern high-speed cameras, Jay snapped away—trying to decipher the mystery of Hogan's hands at impact. Interestingly enough, Curt Sampson wrote in *Hogan* that following the clinic, Hogan asked Jay for a ride to the train depot where, without announcing his intentions, Hogan began his journey to Scotland to play in The Open at Carnoustie. It is interesting to note that these pictures were taken just days after Hogan's im-

pressive U.S. Open victory at Oakmont, and only weeks before his decisive win at Carnoustie. Therefore, we must acknowledge that these images caught the master at work at the peak of his career. (We are grateful that Jean-Paul and his brother Jason believed the photographs would serve history more favorably in a book rather than a bureau drawer.)

And, after all those years, here are those images from the past for us to view.

Notice how Hogan's leg drive and hip rotation force the chest around to face the target. The hands, attached to the Magical Device, are along for the ride until about one foot from the ball. This is where the left hand twists into the secret move, and this short action is really the only movement of the hands from the top of the backswing to the top of the follow-through.

The golfer squeezes the last three fingers of the left hand, as if making a fist, as he arches his hand into the ball. The long left thumb points down to the ball.

In this simple action the elbow dimple remains looking skyward. Only the left hand moves.

The role of the right hand

The right hand is dorsi-flexed (concave) at address and maintains this position at the top of the back-swing. As the Magical Device tilts to drop the hands into the "slot," the left hand begins to turn with its twist and arch into palmar-flexion. The right hand resists, by squeezing the left thumb with the last two fingers, and maintains a strong dorsi-flexed position. The thumb and forefinger of the right hand are, by comparison, relaxed. The left hand dominates the hand action and also controls the club. The right hand unifies the hands with the squeeze by the last two fingers.

Until you develop the hand strength of a professional, you had better forget Hogan's lament, "I wish I had *two* right hands to hit it with."

Any attempt to add speed and/or distance to a shot should be done by speeding up the torso turn with well developed core muscles of the abdomen and hips, or by a last-second emphasis

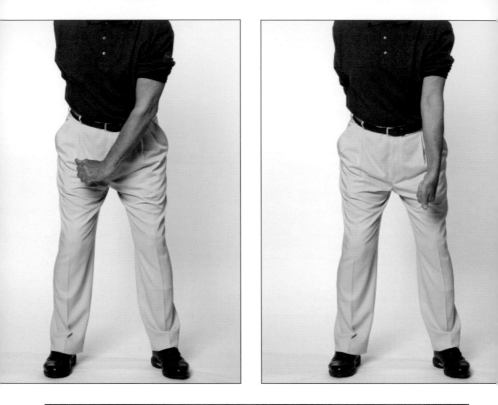

on arching the wrists into the ball. The danger is that amateurs are vulnerable to overpowering the left hand with the naturally stronger right hand, making the left wrist collapse.

The golfer's right hand takes a dorsi-flexed (concave) position at the top of the backswing and holds it as the right elbow returns to its contact with the right hip. As the left hip turns the upper body into the ball, the right hand maintains its concave form and is moved into the hitting zone only by the turning of the stronger muscles of the hips and torso.

Through the ball after impact, the right hand keeps its position, still moved by the body action for both hands throughout the impact zone. The only thing that moves within the Magical Device is the left hand, from dorsi-flexion into palmar-flexion about one foot from the ball. It happens just as the right hip—where the right elbow connects—drives the arched right hand through the ball.

The hands do not pronate or supinate. They are driven through the ball by turning the upper torso toward the target. The arms are firmly connected to the torso. Both hands are arched through the ball and are held in place by the Magical Device, which is powered by the rotation of the torso. Pointing

the left arm's inside dimple to the sky prevents the forearm from rolling over further, and thus prevents a hook.

As the left wrist arches, it forces the right hand to arch as well. At impact, both thumbs point down to the ball in the arched position, giving tremendous structural strength to the blow.

The strength of the hand position is readily observable in this take away by golfing savant, Moe Norman, opposite to the dorsi-flexed (collapsed) left wrist of the uninformed below.

The action of the hands: summary

The right hand is dorsi-flexed (concave) at address and maintains this position at the top of the backswing and throughout the swing through the ball. From the top, as the Magical Device tilts the left shoulder upward, the right shoulder drops the hands into the "slot." At this point, the left hand is also concave in dorsi-flexion.

(Courtesy of RCGA)

(Courtesy of Todd Graves)

At impact, the left hand is in palmar-flexion. The right hand holds its dorsi-flexion, as can be seen here in the swing of Moe Norman.

As the left hand continues into the impact zone, the wrist begins to arch and turn with a twist into palmar-flexion. The right hand, still concave in dorsi-flexion, resists pronation and arches into the ball with the right thumb pointing at the ball.

From the golfer's point of view, only one knuckle of the left hand can be seen at impact, while the right hand maintains a firm dorsi-flexed position. The right hand arches into impact but does not pronate, and the left hand does not supinate. The left elbow, held with the dimples pointing skyward, prevents any roll toward the target by the left or right fore- arms. The entire Magical Device turns toward the target because of its connection to the golfer's torso.

Some details to remember for practice

1. Coming into impact, the left thumb "snaps" the wrist into its arch as the last three fingers of the left hand squeeze into palmar-flexion.

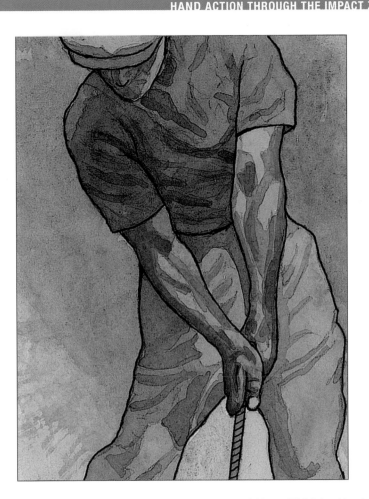

This structurally powerful impact position, demonstrated by a Bill McLuckie sketch, was the centerpiece of Hogan's Magical Device. His hands are posed in the second and final stage of the left hand's secret twist within the Magical Device. This subtle action, accompanied by the fixed position of the left arm, produced the power fade. He wrote that the action for impact was developed by pronation and supination—an inaccuracy that became the source of much confusion because that was not the action he used. The Magical Device is attached to the rotating torso. Only the left hand moves from concave (dorsi-flexion) to a convex position (palmar-flexion) in the space of approximately one foot.

(Courtesy of Jules Alexander)

After impact, Hogan's chest and belt buckle continue to rotate toward the target. The hands remain in impact position into the full follow through.

2. The right hand is held in the concave (dorsi-flexion) position and is pulled into its arched position by the twisting of the left hand.

3. The elbows hold their dimples toward the sky, thus preventing the forearms from rolling on their own. The arms operate as a unit within the Magical Device, which is powered by the torso.

4. For more speed into impact, strengthen your abdominals for a faster turn to the ball. Strength will give you the option of more speed in the movement of the Magical Device. Do not try to swing the arms independently—hold the connected Magical Device unit together and turn the torso with controlled power.

Getting the feel for it

Probably the best way to "feel" the action from dorsi-flexion to palmar-flexion of the left hand is to concentrate on the left hand during the action of a pitch shot—with a half swing away from the ball, and a half swing through impact. The upper body turns away from the target over a flexed and stable right foot (with the weight on the "inside edge"). Mr. Hogan urged his readers to try the drill below as a warm-up on the first tee.

After a free swing back and forth, the golfer will feel the weightless, effortless change in the left wrist as the secret is applied. The torso turns toward the target with the upper left arm connected lightly at the armpit. The right elbow is attached like a fulcrum at the point of the right hip, and the shoulders tilt, rotating on this point. Squeeze the last three fingers of the left hand and twist.

The inside dimples of both elbows remain pointing to the sky. You should not supinate the left hand or the left forearm. If you do, it would be a "flip," and you would have no idea where

the ball might go. If you pronate the stronger right hand, it will likely over-power and collapse the weaker left wrist, and your distance will be reduced significantly.

Alternatives to the Magical Device

There are, of course, highly success-ful PGA Tour professionals who do not employ Hogan's Magical Device.

There are also highly successful players who have developed their own version of the hands at impact position the same way Hogan did, by beating balls every day until they found some-thing they could depend upon.

I met Lee Trevino at Pebble Beach during the Bing Crosby National Pro-Am in 1985 and was pleasant-ly surprised by his enthusiasm for Canada. He had, of course, won the Canadian Open in 1971 by beating the great Jack Nicklaus by one shot in an eighteen-hole play-off at Richelieu Club in Quebec.

The Canadian fans loved the deter-mined little man called "The Merry Mex,' and even more so in 1979 at Glen

Vijay Singh demonstrating his hand position at impact.

Bob Clampett models his hands at impact.

Arnold Palmer.

Abbey when he defeated Tom Watson, who became miffed at the gallery bias for Trevino. Of course, Canadians viewed Trevino as "all American." The kind they like best: happy-go-lucky, friendly, and confident. This was Trevino all right.

Trevino was full of fun in public, but he, like Hogan, had a curse. Super Mex had a nasty, darting hook and, like Ben Hogan, worked hundreds of balls a day learning how to control it. As he often mused, "You can talk to a fade. A hook won't listen."

He also liked to watch Moe Norman practice. One day he passed Moe a new four iron and asked what he thought of it. Moe gave it a waggle, then handed it back. "Too light," he remarked, shaking his head. "Piece of shit. Too light." But Trevino persevered, and coaxed Moe into hitting four shots with the "too light" four iron, which all came to rest within a couple of feet of each other. Now it was Trevino who was shaking his head as he went back to his daily regimen of hitting eight hundred balls.

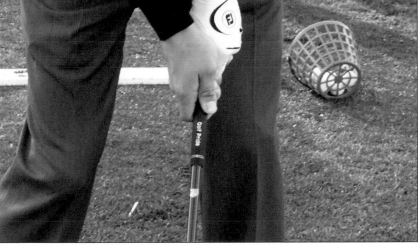

Lee Trevino demonstrating his hand position at impact.

It was on the practice fairway, by trial and error, that Trevino discovered the convex left wrist—which he held from the top and long through the ball—hanging on to the handle for a cut fade with which he won so many titles including the U.S. Open and British Open in the same year (1971) as the Canadian Open.

When one considers what Trevino accomplished with a cut, and that Jack Nicklaus won eighteen majors with the fade, perhaps Ben Hogan's power fade is the way to go. It just takes quite a bit of practice if the golfer does not have a structure as a guide. With Hogan's system, consistency is within reach without a professional's practice regimen.

The object of practicing the secret of palmar-flexion at impact is that it must be absorbed as a reflex action, because the golfer should not be thinking "mechanics" while swinging the club.

On the course, the target must be the key thought. Fortunately, palmar-flexion and the three-finger squeeze with an arch can be practiced on a bus coming home from work, and with that kind of repetition, Hogan's secret practice will soon become a natural action.

Take some half shots with the pitching wedge. Then move to the three-quarter swing. With these longer shots you will notice that the left hip clears away from the target line as the left shoulder moves up and the right knees move under the ball toward the target. Balance on the flat left foot is supported by strength in the left thigh and hip.

CHAPTER 10

THE FULL SHOT

From the address position, Hogan tilted the Magical Device into motion by pushing his left shoulder down toward the ball. It was a nice rhythmical move he practiced during his pre-shot waggle. This pushing movement, in turn, moves the hands away from the ball with arms parallel to the target line, to waist high, where both wrists cock into a dorsi-flexed (concave) position. Then as the hands reach the top of the backswing, the right elbow is pulled upward and away from the right hip. The left shoulder and chin point behind the ball.

The foundation for impact

The foundation for Hogan's Magical Device sets into position during the downswing. This foundation develops as the independent left knee moves over the big toe of the flat left foot, followed almost immediately by turning the steady right knee

toward the target, and turning the hips counterclockwise while in a sitting position—as on a bar stool. Sam Snead worked with his feet to start his knees and hips in this counterclockwise rotation through the ball.

A lot is going on within the split second before impact, but when you get the "FEEL" of it, you can practice in the swivel chair in your office—as a matter of fact that's a great place to develop the feel and understanding for when to apply the palmar-flexion that was the hidden secret within Hogan's Magical Device, because you get to "feel" the role of the feet and knees rotating counterclockwise through the ball—even before the hands reach the top of the backswing.

Necessary drill

Apologies for the next bit of paralyzing (and somewhat repetitive) detail, but this is what you have to ingrain in your subconscious to achieve full control at impact. You should be able to visualize this sequence

and go through it in slow motion. I have a hall carpet leading to a carpeted stairway, and I can enact the process while chipping during idle moments. Five minutes here is very worthwhile.

Just before impact, with the hands about waist high, the dimple of the left elbow is pointing skyward. From here the left-hand palmar-flexion occurs with the squeeze of the last three fingers. The back of the left hand bulges toward the target. Downward pressure on the left thumb forces the wrist to arch so that the thumb points to the ball at the instant of impact.

The left forearm does not rotate toward the target. The left hand snaps into the arched position at impact, and pulls the dorsi-flexed right hand into an arch so that both thumbs point to the ball at impact (as in the address position). Both knees remain flexed. The hands do not turn over after impact (left doesn't supinate; right doesn't pronate). The elbow dimples pointing skyward prevent a rolling over or "flipping" of the left hand and arm.

Feel the upper arms squeezing hard against the ribcage. The abdomen is tense. This is not an "arm shot"—it's a "body shot," and doing abdominal crunches during television commercials will greatly increase your core strength and the effectiveness of this action.

From the point of impact, the turn of the hands and arms toward the target is controlled by the torso, which moves the hands and arms down the target line. As the follow-through begins, the wrists hold their impact position right through the

(Courtesy of Alvie Thompson)

Moe Norman sitting on a bar stool, feet flat on the ground, weight on the inside edge of each shoe, and looking like a middle linebacker. Nothing is going to deflect this club head from its arc into that ball.

The feet help bring the left knee into position.

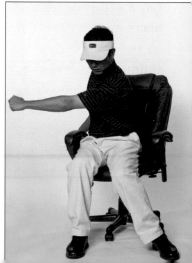

extension, down the target line to waist high, at which point the knees can begin to straighten, and the elbows can bend for the finish position.

The left knee moves out over the flat left foot.

The driving right knee moves under the ball.

The force and power of impact is relative to the strength of the arched hands. (The angle of the right wrist holds its dorsi-flexion firmly, like the right-hand top-spin tennis shot, or better, a top-spin table-tennis shot). This right-hand dorsi-flexion keeps the club face steady through the ball and down the line to the target. And when at address, you assume Hogan's left thumb position—the club face is held a degree or two open—to produce the power fade.

The blow is accelerated for longer shots (say from a half wedge to a three-quarter wedge) by accelerating the raising of the left shoulder which in turn increases the speed of turning the right side (knee, hip, and torso). It is not a lash with the hands—they are along for the ride and are held in their arched position.

CHAPTER 11

HOW THE ACTION BEGINS

At the top of the backswing, the knees remain flexed in the sitting-on-the-barstool position.

Now we come to everybody's favorite question: What starts the downswing to the ball? And we can argue all night about this because feet, knees, hips, and shoulders come in pairs, so it is difficult, if not impossible, to claim which one of the pairs is the initiator. Besides, your present swing might be just fine for you and could accommodate Hogan's secret as is.

Hogan had a special move that started him down from the top and into the impact position. He said it was a move by his left hip toward the target to set him up for thc secret to be applied at impact, but, as Tiger Woods has stated, "Feel is not real." Besides, for an amateur who isn't at the range every day, this is a formula for a "slide," which can mean "out-of-bounds-right" or, if the center of the body slides toward the target, worse: a "shank." Here is a useful procedure: don't think "left

hip toward the target." Instead, like Sam Snead—who noted that he looked "bow-legged" just before impact—think "left knee" toward the target.

From the top of the backswing, with knees flexed in the barstool-sitting position, the left knee shifts from pointing at the ball to moving out over the left foot. This quick and isolated move establishes the foundation for the inevitable weight shift onto a flat left foot.

On the backswing the left knee turns in toward the ball but the right knee does not move from its stable address position, with weight on the inside edge, until it is time to begin the downswing to the ball.

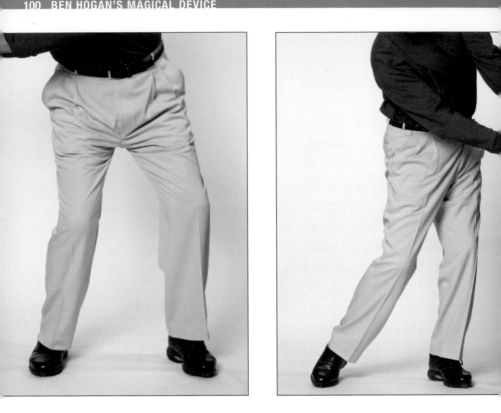

So, the very first move from the top is likely the left knee moving over the stable left foot while the shoulders keep stretching to the top. This move produces an extra half beat in the timing: instead of a slow count of "one" from the address position to the top, and a fast "two" down to impact, the count is now a long, slow "onc" to the top then a half beat. Then a fast "two." One ... bump, two!

The bump is the move the left knee makes from pointing toward the ball at the top of the backswing to its position over the flat left foot.

From that stable position, the golfer is ready to release all muscle tension into the ball. The Magical Device tilts, the left shoulder thrusts upward, and the right side comes pouring through, driving the hand structure into the ball. When the left knee is flicked into place over the flat left foot, the left hip turns in an accelerating counterclockwise direction over the flexed left knee, and this action triggers a driving release of the heretofore stationary right knee.

You can practice this feeling in a swivel chair.

Even the action of imitating the backswing in a swivel chair demonstrates that the hips turn to a lesser degree than the shoulders, because the right knee remains flexed and steady as the upper body's shifting weight loads over the inside edge of the right foot. As a result, the clockwise rotation of the hips is lesser than the rotation of the left shoulder, which goes under the chin and past the ball. The shoulders are still stretching to push the hands to their highest position when the hips have reached their maximum.

At that moment, the left knee flicks into position over the left foot as the first move from the top. Then the first accelerating counterclockwise rotation of Hogan's left hip begins. The left shoulder should rise three or four inches (this is the point where Hogan observed that his swing plane changed from square to the target line, to angled-to-the-target line, in a slightly closed position). The hands, with wrists still cocked in dorsi-flexion, drop into the "slot."

The hands are not pulled down by the arms. Instead, the hands and arms remain in their top-of-the-backswing position until they are moved into the "slot" by the tilting action of the Magical Device, or more specifically, the left shoulder moving up. This upward thrust is followed quickly by the left hip turning

Through swing.

counterclockwise on a stable and flat left foot, and the right knee driving hard under the ball.

Once into the contact zone in this ready-to-hit position, the golfer begins to apply the secret twist of the left hand while the hips turn hard to achieve maximum rotation speed. Now you have the setup for a crushing blow by arched hands from a strong, balanced foundation, which is supported by the Magical Device. It is not a wild slash with the arm, but the tilting and turning of a well composed unit.

The release of the tension of the right hip, which has been rotated over the stationary right knee, now thrusts under the ball, along with the right knee. The hips turn with speed. This brings the torso through its rotation so that the belt buckle is turning to face the target. At impact, most of the weight has moved onto the big toe of the left foot.

And the secret has now been applied: the palmar-flexion of the arched left hand turns the dorsi-flexed right hand through the ball in a very strong arched position, which produces a

solid hit. The belt buckle turns toward the target and, at the farthest point of reach through impact, the left arm straightens while the right wrist loses some of its dorsi-flexion during its extension, as both hands extend to the fullest. When you get the feeling of this graceful, effortless new power from the turning torso, you can hardly wait to hit a full shot. You can duplicate the right hand position (which is still in dorsi-flexion) of Tiger Woods as he shows his stuff with a seven iron to the Fifteenth green at Sherwood Oaks.

(Photo by Mike Lilly)

CHAPTER 12

AND NOW THE FUN PART

George Knudson was a great Canadian ball striker who, like Moe Norman, was one of the few golfers whom Ben Hogan would watch, and George studied Hogan keenly. In 1969, Knudson went to extra holes in the Masters, losing to the great putter George Archer. Jack Nicklaus has been quoted as saying that Knudson was "a guy with a million-dollar golf swing and a ten-cent putting stroke." But despite this weakness, Knudson won eight PGA Tour events, the same number as Mike Weir to date. Like Hogan, Knudson got so much fun out of the action of moving the hands into the ball that he became addicted to practice.

In the summer of 1969, I watched George Knudson hitting balls at Point Grey golf course in Vancouver for the CPGA championships. He was the last one out on the range when I got up enough nerve to ask him a question that was torturing me: "What brings the hands down to the impact zone?"

Knudson's answer was short: "Just move the left knee, like this," he said with a demonstration. "Got it from Hogan. Can't wait to get on my big toe and give that ball a whack."

Drill

Take some wedge shots with a three-quarter swing, and feel the trigger point where you should release the taut right side into the ball.

From a square stance, and with a leisurely pace, tilt the triangle so that the hands are at ten o'clock (with your head at twelve and the ball at six). You can feel the left arm connection at the left armpit, and the right elbow fulcrum grounded on the hip. You can imagine a thick elastic band stretching from the outside of the left shoulder, under the left arm, and attached

The image is that there is a strong rubber band attached to the stable right knee and the left shoulder.

to the inside of the stationary right knee, providing weight on the inside edge. Hogan is alleged to have disclosed once to his caddie, "You know why I'm so goddamned good? My right knee never moves until everything's ready."

At the time of release, the left shoulder thrusts up. Imagine it pulling the right knee to start the drive of the right side.

The right knee, hip, and shoulder drive under the ball.

The golfer first moves the flexed left knee toward the target. Then, as the knee arrives over the left foot and the weight begins to transfer, raise the left shoulder up, hard, and drive the right knee, right hip, and right shoulder through the ball as fast as that elastic can pull!

Alvie Thomson, who was also on the PGA Tour, and a Canadian friend of Knudson, confirmed that George had learned this move from Hogan, and how key it was to the timing of the all-important downswing. Irv Livingstone, of *Fairways* magazine, remembers when Knudson, firing a four iron directly at the flag, apparently oblivious to a lake on the left of a tucked pin, explained as the ball flew at the pin, "I can't hit it left."

CHAPTER 13

HOGAN'S SECRET PUT INTO ACTION

A fter the subtle and invisible left-hand action into the ball at impact has been fully ingrained in your subconscious, it is time to let the beast out of the cage in actual play over eighteen holes.

You have made conscious repetitions of the left-hand palmar-flexion, combined with an arched wrist, fifty times per day for at least a week. You have probably found that you can practice the movement one-handed during boring meetings or when watching television. Twist only the left hand away from the ball into dorsi-flexion, then squeeze those last three fingers into palmar-flexion as you arch the left thumb to point down at the ball.

You may also have changed your setup to match some of. Hogan's characteristics, as described in detail in *Five Lessons*.

He was very specific about his preferences: the grip for the power fade; the left thumb down the shaft with the strong, arched left wrist; the dorsi-flexed and arched right hand.

Checklist

1. The stance: knees flexed and pointed slightly inward; weight on the inside edge of the right foot, never shifting to the outside edge.
2. The dimples on the insides of the elbows point skyward.
3. The turn-away from the ball: left shoulder past the ball on a full shot with your back to the target.
4. The plane: Hogan emphasized the plane by describing the take-away under a "pane of glass" so that the shoulders were parallel to the target line on the take-away.
5. The plane changes slightly as the hands drop into the "slot," because the left shoulder then moves up and points on an angle toward the target line. This means that the left shoulder is slightly closed and is closer to the target line than the right shoulder. The right shoulder should never get closer to the ball than that point established by the left shoulder, or you'll be over the top and pulling the ball.
6. The downswing is initiated by a slow and relaxed movement: the isolated shift of the left knee over to a flat left foot, to be followed quickly by the simultaneous thrust upward of the left shoulder, and the firing of the right knee, the right hip, and the right shoulder under the ball. It must be acknowledged that the same effect can be gained by a simple "sit-down" movement followed by turning the navel toward the target with strong core muscles.

7. The left hip turns counterclockwise around a flexed and stable left knee, while the flexed right knee drives the belt buckle toward the target.

8. Impact: knees flexed and moving toward the target; left hand arching into palmar-flexion with the last three fingers of the left hand squeezing.

9. The follow-through: arched hands extending down the line; finish on balance with weight mainly on the big toe of the flat left foot; belt buckle facing the target on point of right toe; left hand still in control of the club (like Arnold Palmer staring at the palm of his left hand in his follow-through).

The reason why you must ingrain the above-mentioned key points is because playing golf while worrying about mechanics is a sure way to lose the farm. You are allowed only one swing thought, such as turning the left shoulder behind the ball, or keeping the left knee flexed through impact. After that, it's all about visualizing the path of the ball to the target. The timing, feel, and rhythm are all inside you. (And you know how to re-view them all during a practice swing.)

I believe that Mike Weir, the 2003 Masters Champion, is getting a little practice feel before he settles in on the vision of the target during his extended warm-up waggle. Mr. Hogan also emphasized the waggle. When you do it as a small practice swing, you can check the plane going back, the relationship of the shaft to the target line, the start of the dorsi-flexion of the left hand, and the feel of dropping the hands into the impact posi-tion. Most importantly, you can feel the point of balance, where it is so easy to squeeze the last three fingers of the left hand so that the back of the left hand bulges into and through the ball toward the target, and the left thumb snaps into the arched position pointing at the ball. You can brush over this critical point a couple of times, feeling the tilt of the triangle. Then, one last thought, the target and the line of flight to where the ball is to land, three feet from the hole. When it does, you smile. When it doesn't, you might glower (like Tiger) knowing you can do better next time because now you know what should be done. Hogan referred to this realization in *Five Lessons* when he advised:

> "Practice the waggle—perhaps ten minutes a day. In this connection, I'd like to add one contingent thought. When the average player gets ready to hit a shot, some days, purely by accident, he does one or two key things correctly. He hasn't the faintest idea what these key things are, but he does them and consequently he plays quite well. On most days, however—on nearly all days, for that matter—he feels very uncomfortable and unconfident as he addresses the ball, and he is completely baffled when he tries to figure out the remedies that will give him that sense of rightness. 'I just don't have it today,' he rationalizes in his bewilderment. 'I just can't feel a thing.' Well, he's got it that day if he checks his grip and stance and waggles properly. He'll feel that he's got it, and he'll be able to use it."

When you practice and ingrain the feel of the Magical Device and then practice the secret action of the hands in the golf swing, you also will have the confidence to come back after an inevitable poor shot because you know what has to be done and you are ready to do it.

(Courtesy of Jules Alexander)

Hogan got the feel for his secret move under everyone's nose. He said his secret was in plain view if you knew where to look.

The core of the secret move is really quite simple and focuses on one hand, the leading hand. Let's use "the left" for reference here.

The hand action can be practiced everywhere (without alarming people). Working a tennis ball, or the steering wheel while driving, increases strength to the "wringing the towel" action. Left-hand palmer-flexion is just waiting for a long bank line-up. Here the arm extends down to just behind the imagined ball—the left hand is dorsi-flexed, with the thumb pointing to the change in your side pocket. Twist and arch the hand into palmar-flexion. Only the hand moves, because the elbow is held steady, dimple pointing upward, and the hand travels only about one foot until the left thumb points at the imaginary ball.

Going through this hand action with dumbbells during television commercial breaks is good, too.

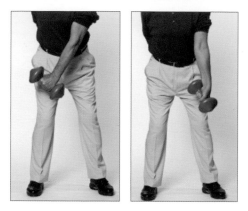

Pause

I would now like to take a moment to emphasize a point about finding a place and a few minutes to exercise, because it became so clear to me how important good strength is for good golf when I slipped on some black ice during Christmas 2007. After three months of nursing a left-shoulder rotator cuff injury, I was barely able to "right hand" it around Monterey Peninsula Country Club for the Boys and Girls Club of America tournament. The strength of my arm was markedly reduced.

Therapy began with exercise in a hot tub, which graduated to swimming. Finally I could lift a two-pound dumbbell, a step up from a can of soup, and I progressed from there. Everything was interspersed with the unpleasant stretching of aging ligaments and stiff tendons. I thought I was done with golf. When I tried to use my left arm with Hogan's secret, the ball couldn't clear my shadow. I remembered that Hogan's leading left hand was his power hand. I was sure it was over.

However, after six months of steady but moderate work (i.e., low resistance, high repetition), I was able to put it back

together—mainly because I knew where to look for my swing.

Hogan's connection at the shoulders was important, and I was able to build up the forearm and hand strength through swing moves with dumbbells, but I found that the old-time golfer's trick of literally "wringing a towel," works wonders.

The left hand squeezes out palmar-flexions by the dozen, while the right hand turns hard in dorsi-flexion.

Probably the best opportunity for obtaining the most repetition for the left hand is to be

The right hand holds hard to its dorsi-flexion. The left hand twists hard into palmar-flexion.

found when driving the car and working the hands on the steering wheel, with the dimples of the elbows pointing skyward, of course. It was a great feeling to hit the ball solidly again by June, and to break my age in the club's senior championship, passing on the way a lot of "pretenders to the throne."

Tiger Woods has demonstrated for all to see that competitive golf is an athletic event and that competitive players had better be strong. What a difference in modern training habits compared with those of, albeit great, golfers like Jimmy Demaret, Porky Oliver, Julius Boros, and for a time, the inimitable Jack Nicklaus.

Hand, shoulder, and core strength allows players the pleasure of planned and controlled hits. It seems to me that even though most of us do not have the time to hit three hundred balls a day as Trevino suggests, we can, however, make the time to do three hundred core crunches at least five times per week. At fifty per minute, that calls for less than ten minutes per session.

One of my "good guy" inspirations is Paul Nemeth, the former wrestling coach at the University of British Columbia. I met him once again a year or two ago at a sports banquet when he was ninety-one. I greeted him by assuming the ready-to-wrestle standing position for Olympic wrestling, and as his wife nearly fainted when he took the strain. I broke off, of course, but was impressed by the power I felt in his shoulders, neck, and arms. "What's your work out?" I asked.

(Courtesy of Mike Lilly)

Tiger Woods at the top of his swing, upper arms squeezing the rib cage, his shoulders stressed over a steady right knee like a catapult about to launch a missile.

"I do one push-up a day without fail," he answered seriously.

When I gave him a puzzled look, he grinned. "One for every year of my life. I get up and do thirty push-ups. Then I shave and do thirty more. Scrub and floss my teeth and do thirty-one. Then I shower and go to breakfast. It doesn't take long."

CHAPTER 14

THE JOY OF GOOD TIMING

L ike romance, the application of good timing for the secret is addictive. There is an elation difficult to explain, but equally difficult to forget. Try to feel the effortless hit through an imaginary ball one more time, as if hitting soft lobs.

As you raise the left shoulder to tilt the Magical Device down from the top to the beginning of the impact zone, take a look. The right elbow is on the crest of the pelvis; the hands are in dorsi-flexion; the left knee is over the left foot; the left hip begins its counterclockwise rotation. And there is a good connection to the torso.

The shoulder raises a bit more and moves the left hand down a few inches further, and brings the right hand almost straight down over the right knee. There is a line-up of the right shoulder, right hand, right knee, and right foot. This alignment should be close to the moment of balance. The left elbow dimple points to the sky and the left palm twists and arches just as the entire right side turns under the ball to the target with the back of the left hand now arched through the ball.

A squeeze of the last three fingers of the left hand should be almost effortless because you have found the balance point. This is where the magic comes from in the Device. Everything happens when the hands find this point. It is a moment of harmony in the universe. No wonder Hogan and his followers became addicted.

The center of the chest (some prefer to think of the navel) turns with the connection between the left shoulder and the torso so that the hands can easily hold their impact position as they swing under the chin, through to less than waist high. This is a position

similar to, but opposite from, the first stage of the take-away from the ball. On the take-away, the left hand is in dorsi-flexion at the waist. On the forward swing it is in palmar-flexion.

When the left shoulder comfortably reaches its highest point, the shoulders begin to square to the target along with the belt buckle, and the hands lift to the finish.

If you can skim through all that in your mind, or swing without a club, and can feel the sensation of the ease with which you can twist and arch your left hand, then you are ready. Take ten minutes before dinner and hit some lobs in your backyard, feeling the point of balance.

Take five minutes and practice finding the 'point of balance'
whenever you can.

The Magical Device on top of a great foundation: the driver

Ben Hogan began his pro tour career hitting his driver hard, and, as a "hooker," he paid the price—as do all players who give the ball a great lash with the right hand, then come close to panic while standing on the eighteenth hole at Pebble Beach, where the largest lateral water hazard in the world looms on the pull-hook side of the fairway.

But Ben Hogan had ingrained his secret in his subconscious and stood on the tee with great confidence knowing precisely where the ball was going. So did Moe Norman.

Moe Norman was the golfing savant who hit thousands of golf balls a day and was confident enough to declare, after Ben Hogan watched him practice, "There are only two golfers who can hit a ball solid every time. Only two—Ben Hogan and me."

He might have been right. Tiger Woods was quoted in *Golf Digest* as saying, "I want to own my own swing. Only two players have ever owned their golf swings. One was Ben Hogan and the other was Moe Norman."

Unfortunately for Moe Norman, despite being a true golfing savant, his sometimes bizarre behavior off the course made him an embarrassment to some, and he missed a lot of opportunities to amaze the world. Augusta National, for example, withdrew his invitation to the Masters when he was discovered sleeping in one of the sand traps. Also, he had taken to entertaining galleries by hitting practice shots off empty coke bottles at the Augusta range.

Every contemporary golfer has a Moe Norman story. Sam Snead used to enjoy telling about a practice round in Virginia when

Moe pulled out a driver on the eighth hole where a creek mean-dered across the fairway 235 yards from the tee. Sam cautioned him to lay up. "I'm goin' for the bridge," Moe declared, "goin' for the bridge," and ran his ball across the ten-foot-wide structure.

Stan Leonard remembers Moe leading the BC Open in Vancouver. Moe was standing on the twelfth hole at Marine Drive, preparing to putt for an eagle, when Stan came to the adjoining second tee. Both men were followed by large galler-ies, and while the onlookers were settling into place, Stan nod-ded over to an adoring Moe Norman, who gestured for Stan to hit first. The usually cautious Leonard waved his thanks and asked, "How's it going Moe?" He immediately regretted his conversational question.

Moe held his putter as a phallus and, waving it in the air in front of him, shouted, "Really good, Stan. Really good."

Stan Leonard, like the spectators, looked frantically for a place to hide. Moe couldn't understand the confusion he had caused, but he certainly understood how to hit a ball. He knew Hogan's secret.

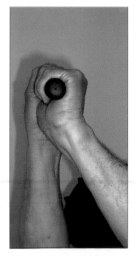

Moe's swing was extremely difficult to analyze because he swung so quickly after placing the tee in the ground and with such speed that it was over before any observer could actually have any hope of seeing what went on. Hogan declared that he could tell if a golfer was going to use his secret by watching the left hand position at the top of the backswing.

Moe Norman's hands were also in the perfect power fade position at address. The rest of his setup was unique, but Hogan liked his hands.

I had the pleasure of "looping" for Moe Norman on his visit to Point Grey for the BC Open, and caddied several times in the same

foursome during the CPGA tournament. Later, I had the thrill of playing with the maestro in Victoria for a BC Open Pro-Am. My putter got hot on the front nine and, after shooting a thirty-two, I found myself ahead of Moe by two shots. He complimented me, but his unusual situation obviously caused him grief, and he kept repeating, "Amateur shouldn't beat a pro ... amateur shouldn't beat a pro."

On the inward nine Moe shot a twenty-nine with seven birdies, and was somewhat relieved with his sixty-three. "Pipeline" Moe Norman was never far from the geographic center of the fairway. For him, the world—or at least the golf world—was back in balance.

The big prize for me came that evening at the Uplands putting green. Moe, characteristically a loner, finished a dinner by himself and then hurried out into the twilight to chip and putt until dark. I had watched him do this many times years before, at Point Grey. There was usually a pyramid of balls in every cup and a trail of empty Pepsi bottles around the green by the time he finished.

Perhaps he had somehow accepted me, because when I cautiously asked, "Could I shag for you Mr. Norman?" I was surprised to hear his reply. "Sure, sure. That'd be good." It was here he showed me his chips, lobs, and pitches. "Here, watch this, watch this. Hands like Hogan. Hands like steel. Just a little tip. In she goes."

Like a great many golfers who were amazed at Moe's ball-striking abilities and saddened by his economic misfortunes, I was grateful to hear that in 1995 Wally Uihlein, President of Titleist and Footjoy Golf Corporation, saw fit to arrange a $5,000-a-month stipend as a gesture to Moe Norman's loyalty to Titleist products throughout his career. It was also good news when the Royal Canadian Golf Association honored the legend of Moe Norman by inducting him into the Golf Hall of Fame in 1992 after a career of at least fifty-five victories on the Canadian Tour. In Jason Zasky's magazine article appropriately entitled *The Greatest Golfer the World Has Never Known*, Moe gave a last quote:

"They're trying to track Old Tiger down already. A lot of guys aren't glad that he's doing well. He's putting a lot of money in their pockets but they don't see it that way. It's awfully lonely at the top," he said. "Nice to be there though."

A review of some of Hogan's support structure for applying the secret to the drive

1. Hogan took a slightly "closed" stance at address, no doubt to reduce the possibility of "coming over the top" with the driver. The ball was positioned in the same place just inside the left heel for every shot—the left foot was moved slightly toward "square" as the club shafts became shorter with a higher-numbered club. And for wedges, the left foot had assumed a slightly "open" position—but the ball was in the same place.

2. His right foot was perpendicular to the target line at ninety degrees with the weight of his foot on the "inside edge." The weight never moved onto the outside of the right foot so that the arc of the swing remained in place, with no swaying movement of the right knee or sideways movement of the right hip away from the target. Senior golfers might experiment with turning the right foot open to 110 degrees in order to make certain their left shoulder reaches (or passes) the ball at the top of their backswing.

3. On the backswing to the top, the left shoulder moves past the ball. If the left shoulder is pointed to the target

line in front of the ball, rather than at ball, the shot will be pushed to the right.

4. The first move down from the top of the backswing is the movement of the left knee toward the target. This maneuver readied Mr. Hogan's transfer of weight onto the big toe of his left foot over a flexed left knee. Tiger, like Snead, uses a little sit-down.

5. When the weight is centered on a flat left foot, the right knee drives under the ball toward the target and the hips turn counterclockwise in a vigorous rotation into impact.

6. The left shoulder is key to establishing the proper plane for the swing so that hand action (arched palmar-flexion) is directed properly into the back of the ball. On the backswing, the left shoulder moves under the chin to a point behind the ball. Then the left shoulder pulls up, skyward. This move drops the hands into the "slot" for a perfect angle to the ball, as the power from the tension in the core is released by a fast turn of the hips. The hands apply the secret, and the power fade is launched.

Hogan's swing exudes grace, balance, and power as the Magical Device turns arched hands through the ball.

(Courtesy of Jules Alexander)

CHAPTER 15

WHAT COULD POSSIBLY GO WRONG, GO WRONG, GO WRONG ...?

Well, you know golf. I think it was Tom Watson who expressed it best, that "a good golf swing is destroyed a millimeter at a time." He was recognizing what we all do—that is, as confidence builds when things start going well, we think we can "get a little bit more out of it." So we begin to increase the speed, or the turn, or something ... and pretty soon the swing is out of kilter, the plane is gone, and the arc is all over the place ... one millimeter at a time.

So ... back to the drawing board. Search out what you have overemphasized or are overthinking. Now, at least, you know what you're looking for. I thought Tiger underlined this confidence when he was interviewed at his Sherwood Oaks

Take note of the position of the tip of the left shoulder at its highest point, and determine never to let the tip of the right shoulder pass over top of that spot. It must stay "under" and never "over."

tournament: "I know how to fix it," he asserted. "I know how to rectify a mistake."

Hogan's tips for problems

Hogan spent a lot of time explaining the correct plane (or angle of shoulders to the target line). At the top of the backswing he gave the image of a pane of glass resting on his shoulders with a hole to poke his head through. This image kept everything in line (parallel to the target line) with the butt of the club pointed to the edge of the ball closest to the golfer. However, on the way down, he wanted the plane to change slightly so that the angle of the shoulders was no longer parallel to the target line but aimed slightly to the "outfield" or close to the target line. The butt of the club must still point down to the "infield" between the golfer and the ball, however.

How did Hogan get there? As the left shoulder is thrust upward, the hands drop into the "slot," and the right elbow regains contact with the right hip. As a result, the left shoulder has not only moved skyward, but also slightly toward the ball on the target line—and there it is: the new shoulder plane that Hogan wanted. This new plane helped visualize a way to keep from coming over the top and double-crossing all of his good intentions.

The new plane is encouraged by Hogan's right elbow— bent and touching his right side—so that there is a definite difference in the height of the shoulders and their distance from the target line.

Turning the right shoulder under the left shoulder point feels a bit as if the upper body is backing into the ball until the

right shoulder and right side pass under this spot. Corey Pavin practices this and refreshes the feeling while waiting for his turn on the tee.

With this position half way down from the top—plus Hogan's secret—you can hit the ball as hard as you like. As Hogan said, "I wish I had two right hands to hit it with," to which he could have added, "after I get into that perfect position half way down to the impact phase." This is when you pour on the power. Before that, the tempo is moderate and purposeful.

Shanking

Shanking a golf ball has so many people terrified that they won't even talk about it, let alone call it by name. Worse, they won't examine its cause, and therefore cannot fix it.

Peter Dobereiner, the great raconteur, told of a French assistant professional named Philippe Porquier who was desperate to earn his Class A certificate in order to become a head professional. All he had to do was prove his prowess in competition, and his confident boss entered him in the French Open at the prestigious La Baule course not far from Brest on the north west coast of Brittany.

The first round went well, and Phillipe was in the lead with greens running fast and true. On this perfect summer day, a two-shot lead going into the fifteenth hole of the final round looked unassailable even after Phillipe faded his three wood—just a touch—up the hill on the par five ... perhaps indicative of a slight slide into the ball.

For whatever reason, it was here things began to unglue when the aspiring Frenchman shanked his third shot over the

fence, losing his ball for a stroke and distance penalty. Shaken, Phillipe dropped another, bore down and shanked his fifth into the rough, mercifully short of the out-of-bounds stakes.

He played his sixth shot only to hear the sickening clack of a shank as his ball flew out-of-bounds again, so he would now be playing eight from the same place perilously close to the boundary fence, over which the next shot flew, as if ordained. His tenth shot followed, while his insensitive caddie remained out-of-bounds, waiting for the next shot. However, the aspiring Frenchman managed to advance the ball to a spot still forty yards from the flag and just past the danger of out-of-bounds.

In spite of this out-of-the-blue curse, the aspiring Frenchman was calm to the point of arrogance while addressing his twelfth shot, but with the ensuing shank, his eyes grew wide as he marched to his ball. He tried to wet his lips, but there was no saliva. He shanked again, and his club ripped open a wide swatch of earth as if searching for the demon infecting his ball.

Somewhat enraged by this unlikely chain of events, which saw him tumbling down the leader board from first place, the now angry golfer aimed once more at the pin, so close and yet so far. He lashed at the ball as if it were a rat, resulting in yet another shank.

Then the gallery did something despicable as he addressed his next shot: from a position in front of him and to his right, they moved en masse behind him and to his left. His face darkened, but sure enough, he shanked his fifteenth. With the silent gallery repositioned, his sixteenth shot sounded the tell-tale clack as everyone cringed in silent suffering for the young golfer, reduced now to shoulder-slumping despair. Subdued, he continued to shank his way around the green with no relief in sight until finally, in desperation, he adjusted his stance to aim not to the pin but to the next tee on the far left of the green. The gallery murmured approval, and when he shanked his eighteenth shot onto the green, they applauded wildly. There was scarcely a sound however, when the haunted man three-putted the slippery green for a record score for one hole on the European Tour: twenty-one strokes!

I would guess that when Hogan said he might have ruined some golfers with his first discussion of the secret, he might have been referring to the timing of the final move into impact when he changed his left wrist from "dorsi-flexion" (concave) to the powerful position achieved with palmar-flexion (arched and bowed). Hogan arched the back of his left hand with palmar-flexion in the split second before impact. If you are slow with this timing, and you have allowed the butt end of your club to point over the ball to the outfield beyond the target line, it's "good-night Irene" as the ball rattles off the hosel into the neighboring postal zone to your right.

Point the butt of the club at the ball.

Note the straightened right knee and the splayed right foot, which encourage problems. When the club points to the outfield the hands are pushed closer to the ball.

If the butt end of your club points over the ball to the outside of the target line, you're flirting with disaster. If you move the center of your body (sternum) slightly past the ball toward the target, disaster can and will strike.

The shoulders should not duplicate the movement of the hips. They have separate functions. On the downswing, the left hip turns away from the target line and the target, while the shoulders move in a completely different direction—the left shoulder thrusts upward and does not slide toward the target. The right shoulder goes down and under the highest point of its partner. When this serendipity occurs, the hands are not pushed an inch or two closer to the ball by the right shoulder coming over the top—and good things are likely to happen. Any decent trick-shot guy can show you the startling results when the left

Stay behind the ball on the downswing by raising the left shoulder up, not toward the target. The upward thrust of the shoulder and tilt of the Magical Device keeps your heart even with the ball, where it should be through the entire swing. This model's center is well past the ball.

shoulder moves in concert and on the same orbit as the left hip so that the hands are pushed slightly toward the ball.

Curt Sampson tells a story from the 1970 Westchester Classic when Ben Hogan startled a couple of the lesser-name competitors with a friendly, "mind-if-I-join-you?" type of greeting on the first tee of a practice round. The nervous young pros had the pleasure of watching the master play a three wood to within two feet on the par five twelfth for eagle, only to be shocked into silence on the par three fifteenth when Hogan shanked an iron into the TV tower. Without changing expression, Hogan reloaded and hit the center of the green. No one said a word. No one picked up the first ball. The incident was ignored, dismissed and forgotten.

The good news for amateurs is that nobody says that you have to achieve Hogan's timing. You can experiment with starting the

palmar-flexion of the left hand as soon as the left shoulder goes up and the hands start down. You will find your own timing to suit your own physique and tempo. At the top of the backswing, the butt of the club must be pointing down at the strip of grass between your toes and the ball on the target line—the infield. If the hands have flopped open so that the butt of the club points over the top of the ball and the target line, somewhere into the outfield, may God help you.

Weakness in the left hand

A leading left wrist collapsing into dorsi-flexion at impact is the amateur's curse. Without the proper structure for impact, a hard-driving, pronating right hand collapses the left wrist to produce a wondrous array of shots, none of which is very pretty.

(Courtesy of B.C. Golf Museum)

(Courtesy of RCGA)

Take a look at Moe Norman's grip for strength: arched right hand, cupped in a dorsi-flexion that doesn't change through the entire swing. Just like Ben Hogan's.

Snap hook

This shot is a killer. It not only costs you strokes and distance, it confuses the hell out of the afflicted, and leaks confidence all over the course. "Where did that come from?" the victim asks. "Everything felt great until I looked up and saw the sharp left turn!"

The player takes the club to the top of the backswing and looks fine. He moves his left knee; he feels the security of his left foot; he raises his left shoulder to drop his hands into the "slot," ready for contact, but then forgets to release his right side! He felt so strong and comfortable, his legs stopped so his upper body spun on the planted front leg, flushed the ball on a hard-flying ninety-degree turn to the out-of-bounds stakes. The belt buckle must keep turning toward the target and "outrace the hands" in order to prevent a hook.

CHAPTER 16

THE MAGICAL DEVICE APPLIED TO SPECIALTY SHOTS

How do I draw the ball?

When asked how he hit a draw or a fade, 1992 Masters champion Fred Couples replied simply, "I just think about it."

The viewer knows what shot Couples is thinking about by his inside-to-outside plane, and the bone of his left elbow pointing to his target. Hogan would approve of the right hand and the right elbow on the hip. He would also like Couples' clearing of the left hip, the driving right side with shoulder, knee, and ankle coming under the ball.

This picture shows Freddie Couples ripping a shot down the right side of the sixth hole at Sherwood Oaks in California, at Tiger's invitational.

(Courtesy of Mike Lily)

Fred Couples arrived at Mount Seymour Golf Club for a Pacific Northwest Junior Championship and played a one iron or three wood from every par four and par five. The local members bragged that the slightly uphill eighteenth green at five hundred and eighty yards had never been reached in two. Fred, with the tournament lead well in hand, pulled out "the big dog," then hit a six iron to the back of the green.

Couples' answer about thinking about a draw seemed to me a trifle understated until six o'clock one morning at the polo field which served as the practice range for the Bing Crosby National Pro-Am. I got to ask the great Jack Nicklaus what he was thinking of when playing his best golf. His answer was down-to-earth and, to my mind, a semi-confirmation of Couples' claim for reliance upon watching images from the right side of his brain.

Nicklaus glanced around, checking to see if anyone else was there, and divulged that when he "was on," he could "see an imaginary pencil line" going from the center of his ball through the air in its flight pattern to the target. "It's like cheating," he said with a grin. "My club just follows the line."

Then I remembered watching Nicklaus preparing for the Sunday round, at the 1982 U.S. Open at Pebble Beach, on the putting green the evening before the final round. Nicklaus finished his session with sixty side-hill five footers; thirty from the left, then thirty from the right. As he left the green, I asked, "Still watching those pencil lines?"

"Yup," was the simple answer, but his grin foreshadowed his last putt on eighteen the next day—five feet of slick side hill, and the pencil line must have been visible, because the ball went on automatic pilot. There he was, tied for the lead with Tom Watson who had just pulled a one iron into the terrible greenside rough on

(Courtesy of Burrard International)

Jack Nicklaus holds a clinic under spring showers in 1997 at Nicklaus North Golf Course in Whistler, BC.

seventeen. It appeared that Nicklaus was in line for his fifth U.S. Open title until Watson flopped a sixty-degree wedge into the hole for a birdie two. When Watson also birdied eighteen, Nicklaus walked out onto the green to embrace his friend.

The sequel to this story came a few years later in 1997, when Nicklaus was in Whistler, BC, to open Caleb Chan's wondrous

(Courtesy of Burrard International)

Interview at the opening of the Nicklaus North Golf Course in Whistler, BC.

Nicklaus North Golf Course, nestled on Green Lake at the foot of lofty Blackcomb Mountain, where every vista is empyrean. At the interview session in the new Nicklaus North clubhouse just before his swing exhibition, I asked the travel-worn and somber Nicklaus if, after all these years, he would be willing to share what he whispered in Watson's ear after victory had been snatched away, leaving him with a record fourth runner-up.

Nicklaus began laughing and found it hard to stop. All he could manage was, "Oh no ... no, this is a family show. I probably told him what a good job he'd done," he lied. Whatever he said, the lesson was clear to me: good players can "see" the pencil line track from the center of the ball, curving through the flight pattern and running into the hole as they visualize the success of the shot.

I don't know if Mr. Hogan visualized quite so vividly as Jack Nicklaus did, but the Hawk was famous for his concentration, so we can only guess what he saw. I don't believe he was "all mechanics" because he engrained his mechanics through repetition. Also, when asked why he had taken so long standing over a putt at the Oakmont U.S. Open in 1953 he replied, "because I hadn't seen it going in yet." As Tom Bertrand and Printer Bowler reported in their book, *The Secret of Hogan's Swing*, Hogan was more precise when a friend asked him about changes to be made in the swing for a draw or another specialty shot.

According to Bertrand and Bowler, Hogan, known for his take-it-or-leave-it absolutes, gave his friend one of his famous laser-eye looks and asserted, "Life is too short to perfect one swing, let alone different swings to draw or fade the ball. We are creating a machine, your machine, where your hands are the chuck, and the club is the tool. If you want to work the ball, turn the tool in the chuck. Never alter the mechanics of your machine to alter the direction of the shot."

Stan Leonard showed me that if you strengthen your left-hand grip and aim the bony point of the elbow at the target, then swing with Hogan's hand action, you can hit a nice five-yard draw, but he also stated firmly, "it's all in your head."

In his 1972 "Shell's Wonderful World of Golf" exhibition with Sam Snead, they were putting on rain-soaked greens that were "stimping" about seven, even after the sun came out. The sixty-year-old Hogan drew and faded the ball at will to hit every fairway in perfect position and then hit every green, beating "the Slammer" 69 to 72. The great Masters' champion, Gene Sarazen, emcee for the program, stated with great sincerity, "Mr. Hogan, that was the most quietly brilliant game of golf I have ever seen. You hit every fairway and every green without a bad shot. How do you do it?"

Hogan did not answer, but might have told us that to "power fade," you would use the "long left thumb" with the left elbow dimple pointing up to the sky. For the draw, he might have advised to "change the chuck" by using a stronger left-hand grip with the elbow pointing to the target, and swing with the same palmar-flexion at impact. He would definitely advise us to experiment and to "dig the answer out of the dirt." He found that if he kept his right foot on the ground a fraction of a second longer, the draw would come. But Hogan's secret within his Magical Device was the real answer for his use, because it produced the power fade. As a result, he knew where the ball was going, by taking the left side of the course out of play—and this move would obviate all the devilish punishment from an "over-the-top" hook.

Bunker play

I have not read or heard a detailed description of Mr. Hogan's use of his secret during trap play. When I asked one of his caddies about it, a sudden look of doubt crossed his face and there was an awkward silence. He finally said in wonderment, "I can't remember Mr. Hogan in a trap."

The closest I could come to an answer to my question about Hogan's use of the secret in bunkers was when I bumped into Stan Leonard one day. "How's your game?" he asked in an unguarded moment. I fumbled for an answer: "Not bad off the tee, iffy on the greens, mediocre with the irons, and absolutely, staring-into-hell hopeless in bunkers."

He gave me a searching look and offered, "Maybe we should fix that."

The next morning Stan Leonard arrived at Point Grey's golf shop dressed as if he were about to tee-off at Augusta National: alpaca cardigan, beautiful matching slacks, jaunty cap, and polished maroon brogues.

He checked in with the golf shop as a professional courtesy. When members on the eighteenth green spotted him, they postponed their final putts to come over to shake his hand. Claire Cruise, a resident at Point Grey since the club's inception, joined us as an eighty-year-old groupie, and out we went to the practice area.

In a deep greenside bunker, I took my sand wedge in sweaty palms and listened as the maestro took me through the art of bunker play as if he were dissecting Rachmaninov's Fifth Piano Concerto: the grip just so, feet wriggled precisely into the sand, angles checked, arcs, plane, knees, feet, wrists, shoulders, head, posture, tempo, on and on for almost an hour until the master announced, "OK, practice on that for a week or two, and you should be all right."

Mr. Leonard nodded at my mumbled gratitude, then suggested, "Lemme try one." He had only a pitching wedge and street shoes—he also suffered from vertigo and had no warm-up—but he gave the pin on the elevated green an intense stare from thirty-five feet away, then floated it up there within eight inches of the cup. Claire and I were still applauding as "Stan the Man" waved from the cart as he drove away back to the parking lot.

He had used the secret, which he called "wringing the towel." He did not need a long warm-up searching for the "swing du jour." He had it ingrained and summoned the procedure for his use, with the waggle.

Hogan showed pictures of trap play in his book, *Power Golf,* published in 1948. The photographs clearly show a strong left hand at address. Coming into impact, the image appears to show the back of the left hand bowing toward the target as in palmar-flexion—but the blurred image is not in focus.

Suffice it to say that in bunkers, the Magical Device and its secret works for me to a satisfying level for an amateur. Perhaps it deserves your experimentation when you have a good degree of mastery of its application in chipping, pitching, and full swings.

Noted golf teacher Ernie Brown obviously remembered Hogan's lesson, as we can see the telltale use of the Magical Device and the position of his hands here.

(Courtesy of Doug Brown)

Here is a similar shot for Stan Leonard in a bunker during the 1958 BC Open showing his Hogan technique.

Just for review: a detailed description of the Magical Device

There are several notable characteristics of the Magical Device when Hogan's arms come into the impact zone:

1. The dimple on the inside of the left elbow is pointed skyward.

2. The right elbow is pressed against the right crest of the pelvis. The dimple on the inside of the right elbow is pointed skyward and is as close as possible to the left arm.

Note the action of the Magical Device and hands. Hogan's triangle works the shot while his lower body is quiet. Right hand is still in dorsi-flexion.

(Courtesy of Associated Press)

3. The left wrist is arched with the long left thumb pointing down the shaft at the ball. The back of the hand bulges toward the target.

4. The right hand is strongly arched and is held firmly in the concave position of dorsi-flexion.

5. The unit, called the Magical Device, is held firmly "connected" to both sides of the rib cage by pressing the inside of both the right and left bicep muscles to the torso.

6. The Magical Device is moved with great force, combined with speed, through the ball by a controlled rotation of the torso.

7. As soon as the left knee flicks out over the flat front foot, the left shoulder thrusts upward and signals the right knee and hip to turn under the ball.

CHAPTER 17

DOES HOGAN'S SECRET WORK?

Hogan's superb record using a repeatable fade, even after his terrible car accident in 1949, speaks for itself when one considers his nine major victories in the PGA Championship, the Masters, the British Open, and the U.S. Open. But can others make use of that shot as a regular strategy?

Jack Nicklaus spent thirty years winning on the PGA Tour with his dominant shot being the power fade. Vijay Singh's precision drives also come to mind.

I also have a clear memory of Andy Bean at the Pebble Beach driving range. Early in the morning the big man would take the spot over by the split-rail fence on the far left side where the expensive cars had paid top dollar to park close to the center of things. Andy brought the action a little closer by practicing five irons that soared over the long line of Lincolns, Cadillacs, and

Mercedes, and cut back just over the fence at the last second. He'd giggle like a kid when there was a close call. It worked for him, so after I had finally analyzed how Hogan brought the club head from a cupped or dorsi-flexed position at the top of the backswing to the bowed and arched position of the left hand at impact, I tried it. Very soon, at age seventy-two, I was thrilled to shoot a sixty-nine from the back tees.

Hogan's tips

1. Ben Hogan was not a big man at five foot nine and one hundred forty pounds, but he was very strong; and when it was strategically indicated, he would hit a driver from the fairway. He knew that a driver off the grass went only one way: low and fading, and he used it only when appropriate—in situations with a suitable risk to reward balance.

    Stan Leonard picked this up from his model while playing on the PGA Tour. Paired with Hogan in 1952 at the classically designed Colonial Country Club, they came to the par five, six-hundred-ten-yard eleventh hole, which was about the only hole on the course that would favor a long straight drive. Hogan had said that "a straight ball will get you in more trouble at Colonial than any course I know."

    Well, Stan hit an outstanding drive far down the center between lurking fairway traps, and elected to try Hogan's tip. He slammed his driver off the deck and watched the ball bound between the two bunkers guarding the front of the green. It headed for the pin, lipped out, and

rolled eight feet away, just missing the double-eagle two. He missed the eagle putt, but left the green with a consolation birdie. "Stan, that was a nice four," Hogan allowed on the way to the next tee.

2. Hogan also used the driver when he had a "low and around" shot from under trees—especially on the right side. When there was a chance to hit the green from a wayward drive under trees, Hogan would give it a long study to determine if he could take advantage of the low-to-left flight of a ball struck by a driver, while not risking a high number.

3. Hogan's putting strategy followed much the same line of thinking. Hogan did not want to three putt, and would go through four rounds on tournament slick greens without doing so. He determined where he wanted the ball to come to rest for his second shot if he missed the first—

and that preference would be below the hole with an up-hill shot. With competition greens stimping over twelve, this strategy saves strokes as well as ulcers.

4.   When practicing putting before competition, Hogan would often putt to a tee peg or a dime instead of the hole. Psychologically he figured it was more positive because the hole eludes the ball so many times. There is also the lack of intrusion by finding a quiet moment off to the side of the putting green.

An added benefit during an important putt out on the course is the easy image of your dime sitting at the front edge of the hole and rolling the ball over it in through whatever angle you "see." The player can also imagine the tee peg situated so that the ball would topple the peg into the hole.

Short putts are made easier with a more confident knowledge that when putting to a dime (in your imagination) on say, the left front edge of the hole, the ball would have to break three inches to miss. That is hard to do, and so a golfer strikes the ball more confidently across to an imagined dime.

5. Hogan believed strongly that if the pin is tucked to the right side of the green, the golfer should fade the shot into the pin from the green's center.

6. It follows that if the pin is on the left side of the green, the golfer would be wise to bring the ball in from the center again. Perhaps this was why Lee Trevino would ask amateur partners rhetorically, "Is there anything really wrong with being in the middle of the green?"

7. Fairway bunkers could be annoying, Hogan knew, but he also understood that a steady stance over the ball enabled the golfer to "pick it clean" while secure in the knowledge that "thin" shots always go straight.

    Picking a club with the right loft is easily determined by holding the back of the head of the proposed club close to the ground outside the trap (or very carefully just above the sand to avoid penalty) to look at the line of the shaft. This is called the angle of reflection, which gives a clear picture of the path of a ball struck with a club of that loft.

8. Hogan addressed the ball in a forward position, off his left heel, because he liked to hit the low-numbered clubs high to stop them better on firm greens. Conversely, Hogan would hit high-numbered irons (six through wedge) lower than their lofts would suggest, by moving the ball more

toward the right foot, in order to let them run to the hole like a putt. With similar thinking, Paul Azinger is very good at these shots and called them "punch shots." The 2008 Ryder Cup captain was so accurate that he once remarked, "I should hit these all the time."

9.   Hogan was always very careful about analyzing his lie. If there was a grade to contend with, he would adjust his shoulders parallel to the angle of the ground beneath his feet: he would lower his left shoulder for a downhill lie, and raise it if uphill. When in the rough, the torso and knee action helps prevent grass from grabbing the hosel and redirecting the ball.

(Courtesy of Peter Burnet)

10. When the pin was near the front of the green, Hogan would hit it in high past the pin. When the pin was at the back, he would hit it lower for a run-up to the hole."

11. Hogan knew that the arc made by the club head on take-away must return to the same spot behind the ball exactly, or the shot would be fat or thin because of a lateral sway—hence his stationary right knee with the weight on the inside edge and the question to his caddie: "You know why I'm so goddamned good? Because I never move my right knee going back."

    He knew, too, that there could also be a "fore and aft" sway, and so maintained inside pressure on his left and right heels until impact when the right heel is pulled off the ground.

12. Recovery shots should always be analyzed thoroughly in order to find the best angle to the pin for the following shot. Hogan agreed with Gene Sarazen, who said, "When you play safe, make sure it's safe." However, Hogan improved the strategy by the strategy by playing safely to the ideal position to ensure an "up and down" while avoiding the possibility of a double or triple bogey at the same time.

13. "Don't stand where I can see you!" Hogan admonished all caddies (and more than a few fellow members in Pro-Ams, a caddie reported). "Stand behind me looking at my back, or in front looking at the top of my head."

(Courtesy of Jules Alexander)

Hogan with a line of caddies and an official playing with Claude Harmon. Young caddie Butch Harmon watches carefully from the end of the line.

CHAPTER 18

MORE GOLF STORIES WITH A HOGAN TWIST

The man who worked for Hogan

Kevin Riley was born in 1936 and lived across the street from old Shaughnessy Heights Golf Course in the most fashionable residential area of Vancouver. He could slip under the club's fence anytime he wanted, and thus spent most of his daylight hours caddying or shagging or beating balls himself. When Ben Hogan came to old Shaughnessy for an exhibition match in 1948, Kevin was fascinated by the man's demeanor and determined to make golf his life. And what a life it was, for as fate would have it, he would eventually wind up working for Mr. Hogan, and still does.

When he was seventeen, Riley won the World Junior Championships in Eugene, Oregon. He turned professional and

worked for Rod Funseth and Claude Harmon, learning a lot about golf as well as a great deal about teaching techniques. He was hired as head professional at Fairmont Country Club in Chatham, New Jersey, and began working for Ben Hogan in 1972 as a club representative. Kevin remains with the company to this present day.

I kept track of Kevin, because golf had this strong attraction for me as the chess game of athletics. I was fortunate to play with Kevin one day and listen to him reminisce about Ben Hogan, the golfer he admired so much.

Kevin had never played a round of golf with Ben Hogan, but, of course, had met "the boss" during business meetings. He was thrilled one day to be invited to the Shady Oaks Club in Fort Worth, Texas, for a round of golf with the great man, and the promise of perhaps a drink or two to follow. Kevin dressed smartly and warmed up at the range, only to hear that Mr. Hogan was not feeling up to a game that day. Disappointed, Kevin enjoyed the charming course and afterwards was pleased to hear that Mr. Hogan would join him and Charles Epps for dinner.

He had been told that Hogan held his knife and fork just like he was gripping a golf club in each hand, and Kevin was amazed to witness this idiosyncrasy himself. But it was Hogan's memories that made the visit such a treat. A question about why Hogan had not taken up with the Senior Tour touched a nerve. "They never asked me," came the quick response.

Apparently there was an office oversight, as Mr. Hogan had been contacted only to state that he would be teeing off with his longtime friend Jimmy Demaret as his playing partner in a two-ball tournament in Austin, Texas. "I don't need a partner, and I don't play in putting competitions," was Hogan's chilly reaction.

Kevin pointed out to me that the Hawk had, in later years, become very sensitive about his putting as the vision in his left eye, which had been injured in the 1949 bus accident, deteriorated. This sad state was hard to take by a champion who at one time had played a seventy-two-hole tournament at the tough Oakland Hills course without a three putt. Hogan could still hit sixty-five or sixty-six greens but couldn't putt with guys like Loren Roberts or Brad Faxon anymore.

Kevin knew that, like Snead, Hogan struck the ball very well and rarely three putted. It would be interesting, he wondered, how these two, who dominated golf for such a long time, could have played with modern equipment. "There's no telling what they could shoot," he suggested.

According to Riley, Hogan never believed in gambling—at least not on a golf course. In the bad old days of the thirties, Hogan would go broke trying to scratch out enough tour prize money to stay out on what he hoped could become a "gold trail," and he was always looking for a decent paycheck that could keep him going—like one of his first paydays at Bing Crosby's Clambake in 1935, where he earned the robust sum of seventy-five dollars. Several times he had to drop out to take a job as a Reno croupier or blackjack dealer before he could get back on tour, but he didn't like gambling on the course. The thrill of hitting the ball into perfect position was his challenge.

Kevin recalled that Hogan had, of course, played better ball golf matches with partners before, and was especially fond of one match he played with Byron Nelson at Cypress Point Club near Pebble Beach. The Monterey Peninsula was not at all like the high plains of Texas. This was the place poet Robert Louis Stevenson had called "the most felicitous meeting of land and sea on God's green earth," and Hogan loved it.

Looking from the Cypress Point clubhouse to the landing area for the drive at the seventeenth tee, one of the great unknown holes in golf.

The sixth green at Pebble Beach.

For this Cypress Point match, Hogan partnered with Nelson against amateurs Harvey Ward (1955 and 1956 U.S. Amateur champion) and Ken Venturi (runner up in the Masters as an amateur, and a man destined to win the 1964 U.S. Open Championship).

One stroke down coming back from the ocean to the traditional white clubhouse high on a hill and bordered by cypress trees, Venturi birdied the eighteenth to tie the match. Hogan immediately drained a slippery ten footer for the win. "I don't lose to amateurs," he grinned. He and Nelson had a sixty-one for their better-ball one-up victory.

Unfortunately, the climate of Northern California was found to be too cold for Hogan's wracked body to function well.

The Crosby National Pro-Am at Pebble Beach was held at the end of January and was the wrong time of year for him.

The Hawk still liked Southern California, though, and the Riviera Golf Course that many called "Hogan's Alley" because he did so well there, winning the U.S. Open in 1948 and three Los Angeles Opens in 1942, 1947, and 1948. Playing at Riviera in his first tournament following recovery from his auto accident in 1949, Hogan was leading the tournament until Sam Snead birdied the last hole to tie. He told Kevin that in those days the playoff to break the tie was eighteen holes on Monday. He and Snead liked that, because the custom then was that both contesting players split half the Monday gate with the club. There wasn't a bigger draw than Hogan and Snead at the time, and they wound up getting more for Monday than for winning

Jack Nicklaus' favorite hole—the 8th tee at Pebble Beach.

first prize on Sunday. In 1953 the winner got $2,600 for the win. Tickets for the Monday tie-break were two dollars, and if twenty thousand people showed up, that would give them both an extra $10,000.

Hogan admired Snead's swing, and so did Buck Buchanan, a keen amateur who was a scratch player for forty years. Buck worked for International Flavors and Fragrances and had won four club championships, including Baltusrol and Plainfield in New Jersey. Mr. Buchanan was instrumental in bringing Hogan, Nelson, Bing Crosby, and Bob Hope to South America to play exhibitions in the thirties. He was also the first American to be invited to sit on the Rules Committee for the Royal and Ancient Golf Club at St. Andrews. At age eighty-two, Buchanan could break eighty every round he played.

At this level of authority, it was Buchanan who settled an argument between a golf writer for *The New York Times* and one from *The Washington Post* regarding the best golfers of all time. Buchanan argued that Byron Nelson had ruled golf for ten years; Ben Hogan was the best for twenty years; Nicklaus was on top for thirty seasons; but Snead was on top for life. Kevin believed that Hogan would have agreed with this view of these gifted men.

At the dinner Kevin had with Mr. Hogan, he found Hogan to be caustic about the caddies on today's PGA Tour. "Like a bunch of seeing-eye dogs telling the players what to do," he growled. Otherwise, Hogan loved caddies and would help them out whenever they got in trouble. He was all business, however, when they were working for him. "I want you to carry the bag and give me balls," he'd tell them. "Don't ask any questions. Just stay quiet and let me figure out the next shot."

Hogan also wanted his clubs handed to him by gripping the shaft. "Don't touch the grips or the club heads. I don't want any sweat or skin oil on 'em."

Strangely enough, in spite of Hogan's rigorous control of caddies, he was very generous, even giving some young men with golfing talent free sets of his famous clubs. Another facet of his personality is revealed by the fact that he never kept score. Instead, he made his caddie do it, and checked the card only after the round was completed. During the round he never had the time.

Mr. Hogan was emphatic about these things because he only wanted to concentrate on the next shot. Where was the best angle to the hole? Where is the trouble? Where should the ball land? He was so focused, Kevin recalled, that when Hogan was playing in the Masters at Augusta's famous twelfth hole—defined by Hogan himself as the hardest par three on tour—the Hawk put in a clever shot that resulted in a birdie two. Claude Harmon, one of Kevin's former employers, aced the hole—one of the few in Masters history. Hogan spoke not a word. He referred to Harmon's shot only tangentially on the next tee when he said, "Claude, I think it's your honor."

Stories like that are not to indicate that Hogan didn't know what was going on in the big picture; it was just that he wanted to focus completely and without distraction on his own play. During a competition at Riviera in a threesome with Marty Furgol and another tour player, Hogan had watched the tour player take practice swings while in the trees. After holing out, Hogan asked the player, "What did you have?"

"Four," the man replied, to which Hogan shook his head.

"You broke a twig—two strokes." The player argued that he had not changed his lie by breaking a branch, but Hogan was

adamant and would not sign the card—he was that sure of what he saw—as well as his knowledge of the rules of golf.

In 1955 Mr. Hogan went to the Pro-Am for the Los Angeles Open at Inglewood Country Club. Kevin sat with Lloyd Mangrum and remembers a shot Hogan made at the par-four eighteenth hole. The final hole had an elevated green with approximately eight degrees of slope to receive the second shot. Hogan appeared to be in big trouble when his ball took a strange bounce and went over the back of the green and down a slight hill. With the gallery watching anxiously, Hogan chipped from over the back of the green to a putting surface sloping away from him. The ball took one hop next to the hole, at which point it bounced past the cup, then it put on the brakes and backed up the eight-degree slope, stopping within two feet of

(Courtesy of Associated Press)

Hogan's hands are still in control of the club face after teeing off in the rain for the Open in Carnoustie 1953. Cecil Timms, his caddie, looks to be enjoying the show after eating Ben Hogan's candy found in the bag.

the hole. Kevin had been sure the ball would roll over the front edge of the green for sure, but no, it was another spectacular shot. "That's Hogan," Mangrum said. "He does stuff that no one else can."

Kevin, however, was reminded of the Canadian Open at old Shaughnessy in 1948 when Mangrum had played out of trouble with a billiard shot off a tree and onto the green of the par-four twelfth hole. "Mr. Mangrum, who won the Los Angeles Open five times, was also something." Kevin knew. "But Ben Hogan stood alone," he concluded, "the best of the best."

The oldest-playing Hogan practitioner

This syrupy swing belongs to Charles Hillman who, at ninety-one years, breaks his age regularly. He began studying Ben Hogan's *Five Lessons* fifty years ago and highlighted many of the good bits to refer to now and then. He also studied Jim Ballard voraciously—the man who emphasized the power inherent within Hogan's connection of arms to the body.

Charles takes a golf lesson once a month—whether he needs it or not—and stays loose with daily Tai Chi and ballroom dance lessons once a week. If you think his swing looks good ... you should see him ski Whistler.

A biographer's view

On a brittle February day in 1922, Hogan's father shot himself in the chest in front of his nine-year-old son, Bennie. It is reasonable to assume that this shattering image shaped Hogan's observation of the world and rationed the amount of trust he could assign to people. Perhaps this shocking event would also explain why so many tour professionals who played with Hogan felt that, although they knew him, they never really did understand him. Jimmy Demaret tells of the time he came across Hogan lunching alone, as usual, and made the dark joke, "Here's Ben Hogan dining with all his friends."

The Great Depression of the "Dirty Thirties" scarred many men, but this is not to say that Ben Hogan was without charity. The biography by James Dodson, *Ben Hogan: An American Life*, points out in fascinating detail Hogan's awareness of people down on their luck and his capable analysis of the difference between those who were trying to take advantage, and those who deserved a hand. In one example, Dodson tells of a Ben Hogan who stopped a young man named Mike Wright, an assistant professional who was to interview for the head professional's job at the tender age of twenty-three, as he arrived at Shady Oaks course the day of the interview. Hogan posed a few questions before asking Wright, "You got a jacket?"

"No, Sir, I don't," answered the young man.

"Well get over to the store and buy one on my account."

When the young pro graciously turned down the offer, Hogan shrugged off his own jacket, "Here," he offered, "take mine." That's the way Hogan was.

Stan the Man

Stan Leonard often played with Hogan, but always in competition where Hogan rarely spoke. Stan looked pained when remembering the day his idol asked him to play a practice round. Leonard was put on the spot because he had made other firm plans and declined, "Sorry, Ben, I've made some appointments. Let's make it some other time."

Hogan's eyes became distant. "He never asked me again," Stan lamented, shaking his head. "I could have cancelled those other guys ... but that wouldn't have been right."

When the Hawk stares you down

Alvie Thompson and Jeff Buder, both Canadian professionals, remember when George Knudson met Ben Hogan, the man after whom George was trying to model himself.

George had been invited to meet Mr. Hogan at the Colonial Golf and Country Club for a drink and a chat, because Hogan admired Knudson's swing and recognized the Canadian's potential. Perhaps it was forgotten that Knudson was a rather free spirit, and that the seventies were a bit slack on dress and etiquette. Anyway, no one spoke to Knudson about decorum, and so he arrived a little late wearing cowboy boots and blue jeans, all topped off with a mass of curls above a wide grin.

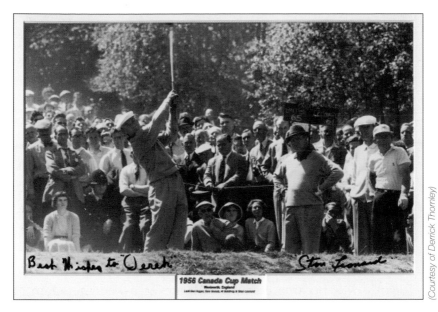

(Courtesy of Derrick Thornley)

Ben Hogan tees off at Canada Cup Championships in Wentworth, England before a spellbound crowd. Sam Snead is watching closely, but Stan Leonard is thinking about something else as a young Al Balding lurks self-consciously in the background while in the presence of such famous fellow competitors. As fate would have it, the Canadian team won by beating the best twosome in the world.

The smile disappeared in a hurry when Mr. Hogan turned on him with a glare and a simple message, "Get out of here and freshen up. Don't come back until you look like a professional."

George was back in an hour with a shave, a haircut, and a nice navy blue blazer with gray slacks. Knudson offered a cigarette to Mr. Hogan. "Care for a Canadian cigarette?" he asked casually. Hogan looked him up and down then reached for the case. "If they're as smooth as your swing—I'll try one," and the friendship began.

Summer at Jasper Park Lodge, 1953

Ross Collver was a starving student at the University of British Columbia who, as a young golfer, was very happy to get a summer job at Jasper Park Lodge, nestled in the towering peaks of the Rocky Mountains near Banff, Alberta. The thought of being able to play the famous Jasper course—one of Stanley Thomson's architectural triumphs—when the course wasn't busy was a special treat, because this was the place celebrities like Bing Crosby and Jack Benny came to savor the scenery far from the madding crowd.

Long distance shot taken from behind as Hogan hits to caddie in Jasper, Alberta.

(Courtesy of Ross Collver)

In August 1953, working as a waiter, Ross couldn't believe the good news that Ben Hogan was coming to Jasper only days after he had won the British Open at Carnoustie. More than that, Ross had the afternoon off and determined to follow "Bantam Ben" for the full eighteen holes with his camera.

Ross was too frightened to go near Hogan, and took photographs discretely from afar.

He would however, be close enough to hear Hogan's only words during that round

while shooting a tidy sixty-eight. Coming to the narrow entrance to the difficult seventh green, Hogan turned to one of Jasper's assistant pros, and speaking for the first time asked, "Can I reach those grassy knolls over there?"

"Not a chance," came the confident answer.

Hogan ripped his drive only to watch the ball bound right into the knolls. He glared at the young man and spoke not another word for the rest of the round.

Big Boy Miller

Roy Miller has been a caddie at Pebble Beach for thirty years and has seen it all. The moments he remembers keenly were the times he shagged for the tidy little man they called "Bantam Ben."

"He was all business," Larry remembers fondly, "and he loved what he was doing. He would hit one irons, and I

(Courtesy of Ross Collver)

Ben Hogan, cigarette in mouth, happily at work. Hitting golf balls while manipulating the curve, the spin and the trajectory . . . monitoring his touch, and always in control of everything including his de rigueur wardrobe which included twelve hundred dollar hand-made shoes from London, with an extra spike in the centre for dependable grip.

never moved more than a step
or two. It was like firing tennis
balls out of a blowgun. I could
get hit!"

"Another thing. He was,
well … nice to me."

The King
comments on Hogan

Big Roy Miller caddying at Pebble Beach.

In his book, *A Golfer's Life*,
Arnold Palmer gives his opin-
ion of Ben Hogan as one rival viewing another. He saw the Hawk
as "now almost more legend than man, but he still ruled golf like
an icy monarch determined not to give up the throne."

Palmer reviewed Hogan's career following the 1949 car crash
and, with the greatest respect, noted that, "Hogan, the most me-
thodical attacker of golf courses of his era—playing six seventy-
two hole tournaments and winning five, including wins at the
Colonial, the Masters, the U.S. Open, and the British Open,
a feat some compared to those of Jones in his prime. If Ben
Hogan's career had a peak, that was it."

On a more personal level, Palmer remembered his awe for
the man, for whose records he would battle. He had played
for Captain Hogan on the Ryder Cup team, and was finally
to play a round with the "monarch" along with Jackie Burke
at Augusta in a practice round arranged by 1958 PGA champion Dow Finsterwald. Palmer had driven all night following a
Monday morning play-off with Howie Johnson at the Azalea
Open. After a painful loss and a late-night drive from Wilm-

ington, North Carolina, Palmer was deflated and tired, and his play reflected his mood.

Following the match, as Palmer was changing, he overheard a remark from Hogan which cut to the bone. "Tell me something, Jackie. How the hell did Palmer get an invitation to the Masters?" Arnie was burned by that jibe and buckled down to win his first Green Jacket in 1958 with the conclusion, "So perhaps I owe Ben a tip of the cap for helping me focus my mind on my business the way Pap always insisted I would have to, in order to win a major golf tournament."

Three men who helped changed the face of golf

Before Ben Hogan became the hottest name in the world of sport, he was invited to an exhibition series in South America to help popularize the game of golf. It was 1938, and times were tough, but he was to be accompanied by two exciting new names in Hollywood: Bing Crosby and Bob Hope. Any of Hogan's skepticism was swept away by the promise of much-needed appearance money with all accompanying expenses covered. Besides, he had been to Crosby's Clambake in 1937 where, at Rancho Santa Fe, Bing pulled people together for the sake of charity while trying to forget the devastation of the Depression for a few days. They sang. They laughed. And they played golf with a unique feature where amateur celebrities—excited beyond stage fright—were partnered with a touring professional. It might be Sam Snead, Jimmy Demaret, or Byron Nelson. Whoever it was, you were teamed for the week, and great friendships were sometimes forged for life.

The winner of the first Crosby Pro-Am was the natural athlete and backwoods boy from Virginia named Sam Snead. When Bing handed him the winner's check for $500, Snead replied, "If it's all the same to you, Mr. Crosby, I'd rather have cash." Hogan won a much-needed seventy-five dollars and was very grateful for it, but perhaps realized that he had earned more than money. The withdrawn Ben Hogan was appreciated for his demeanor and his sincerity, and was treated accordingly by the host. Crosby was fun, he had to admit. But more than that, he was also polite and sincere. Hogan liked the man.

Bob Hope, Crosby's friend and Hogan's other traveling companion on the South American golf clinic tour, was extroverted in front of an audience, with one-liners and often risqué jokes

(Photo courtesy of Associated Press)

Hogan with Bing Crosby in a relaxed
moment at the Clambake.

that Hogan enjoyed. On the course, Hope was serious about golf, and in private, was quiet and thoughtful. More than that, Hogan discovered that Bob Hope came up the hard way and had once tried to eke out a living as a boxer nicknamed Packy East. Hogan could relate to this celebrity who treated him as a friend.

Hogan also heard from the caddies what Hope and Crosby were like: "Crosby was a true four handicap. Hope was a seven. Once when Hope beat Crosby, Bing said he forgot his wallet. A couple of days later Crosby was handed some money as change for a purchase. Hope snatched the money and ran like hell with Crosby right after him. You could phone at two in the morning if you got in a jam. They helped you out, no matter what." Of course, Hogan, the ex-caddie, was the same.

It would seem that Ben Hogan gradually became relaxed enough with other men who had come from the fear and humiliation that poverty provokes, to play the straight man occasionally.

(Courtesy of Associated Press)

Tiger Woods

The symbolism of the new champion, Tiger Woods, in his Sunday uniform of red and black, hot after Ben Hogan's records, is quite apparent as the young champion strides up toward the crest of the Ben Hogan Bridge across Ray's Creek at the twelfth hole at Augusta, Georgia.

It is interesting to compare super-athletes and to imagine them competing against each other—especially if you recognize that under the "Performing Arts Umbrella" Ben Hogan and Tiger Woods are artists playing the most complex game in the world. I suspect that these two golfers, like athletes in the highest percentile rankings of other fields such as Jesse Owens, Wayne Gretzky, Michael Jordan, Babe Didrikson, et alia, would have competed well in any era. How lucky we are who have seen them both.

It is also fascinating to compare the upbringing of Hogan and Tiger as children: Tiger with a solid, well structured two-parent family, and Hogan, who had precious little of that; Tiger with a disciplined former Green Beret as a manly model, and Hogan, whose father committed suicide in front of him at age nine.

Tiger went to Stanford with friends whom he could trust, and from whom he could learn. He developed a remarkable physique and has access to the latest engineering triumphs to be applied to his equipment. Hogan left school early and could trust no one.

Tiger's determination appears to have risen naturally from an interaction with positive experiences and a resulting rising confidence. Hogan's determination, on the other hand, was likely developed within an atmosphere of mind-searing desperation.

It is a constant source of awe for me that two such superb competitors could have risen from such disparate beginnings, and yet both so hungry for mastery of a game more complex than chess. Of course ... isn't that what golf is all about?

EPILOGUE

Ben Hogan stories abound as we look back on the career of this determined champion. Following his retirement from competition, he turned to recreational golf at his Shady Oaks club near Fort Worth, Texas. Of course, fellow members were anxious to play a round with the legendary ball striker. However, when so honored, they were perplexed to find that when Mr. Hogan reached the green, he would pocket the ball rather than suffer the indignity of putting poorly with the clouded vision in his left eye, an impairment that resulted from his 1949 car accident. Others have proposed that Hogan never considered a putt to be in the same category as a golf stroke, so he refused to contemplate the idea that a "ball striker" could lose to a "putter." It was reported that he once told the great putter Billy Casper that Casper would be "selling hot dogs" if he couldn't putt so well. Jimmy Demaret apparently quipped, "Maybe, but Casper would own all the hot-dog stands."

In any case, the members of Shady Oaks were determined to test themselves against one of the game's greatest legends, and thus contrived a game where Mr. Hogan would play the ball from tee to green, and his caddie would putt out. Money was bet on the sly, because Hogan had warned, "If there's money involved, I don't want to hear about it." The match began with several dozen members following along, watching to see if the best ball from three members could beat Hogan's "assisted" score.

The chosen caddie was "Big Harry Cotter," who knew Hogan from Quail Creek Golf Club in Oklahoma. Harry's Dad was part owner, and Hogan liked to visit when he was in the neighborhood. Big Harry played football for the Oklahoma Sooners, was to serve in the Marines in Vietnam, and was a scratch golfer in his own right.

The big-money match is best described by the caddie himself in complete detail, and with appropriately accented dialogue: "From the first tee, par four, 390 yards, Mr. Hogan faded a drive to the right side of center; then he hit a pitching wedge three feet; I made the putt—birdie—one up. On the next hole, par four, 428 yards, Mr. Hogan faded a drive 250 yards then skipped a five iron in eight feet. I sank the putt for a birdie—two up."

The litany droned on to the ninth and final hole where Big Harry had ridden Mr. Hogan's immaculate shot-making for a twenty-nine, with wagers totaling just under $3,000. "Mr. Hogan hit nine greens inside twelve feet—I sank seven of them … and that was enough for the members."

"It was very tough to get Mr. Hogan to play members because he was not a real friendly guy. If he liked you, he'd do anything for you. People thought he was rude, but he just wanted to play golf—not to visit."

Even if we review all of Mr. Hogan's sixty-three PGA Tour trophies and his domination of so many majors that leave us in breathless admiration for the beauty of his shots, like the one iron at Merion in 1950 to win the U.S. Open, there remains one more story that demands our heed. It was related by Mike Wright, the young head professional at Shady Oaks in Westworth Village. He was, very likely, the last person to see Mr. Hogan strike a ball.

As advancing age overtook the great champion to the point where even his practicing dwindled away, it was doubted that he still had the ability to return a controlled club face with power to the ball as he had done for so many years. Mr. Hogan must have wondered that himself because, when closing in on eighty years, he came to the pro shop late one afternoon and asked the pro for his driver and three balls.

Mike obliged and watched from the shop window as the Hawk went to the tenth tee and plugged one in. The hole was 370 yards and well trapped. To open the green to the best angle for a tucked left pin, the drive should be to be right of center and past the fairway traps. Mr. Hogan hit three balls with his signature power fade. He smiled and nodded as they all came to rest beside each other in the perfect spot.

Mr. Hogan then returned to the shop where he handed in his club, thanked the pro with a wave, then left the game forever, passing away in 1997 at the age of eighty-five.

A last word

If you train yourself to do just three things repeatedly without having to think about it while you swing to the target, you will shock your opponents, and they will pay homage to your diligence by handing you money:

1. Start the downswing with a sit-on-the-bar-stool which moves the left knee over top of the flat left foot.
2. Follow that with a hard upward thrust of a strongly connected Magical Device.
3. Imagine that the left shoulder is attached to the right knee so that they move together, along with the right hip and shoulder under the ball as you apply Hogan's secret.

Even when you blunder, you know how to do it correctly next time.

If you take a last look at Bill McLuckie's sketch of Mr. Hogan's image just before impact, you will realize how easy it is to see the Magical Device and the beginnings of its secret within.

Quod Erat Demonstrandum.

Here we can easily see Ben Hogan's Magical Device, and the application of his secret.

ACKNOWLEDGMENTS

S ir Thomas Sean Connery, a golf purist, was the first person (and for a long while the only person) who showed an interest in this book. I now realize that it would have "died a borning" if his encouragement had not been there. Also, I soon came to realize how like Ben Hogan he is. Born in abject poverty, both men rose to the top of their professions by the dint of steel wills and eyes that could burn holes in one's forehead if angered. On the golf course Connery was the same when standing over the ball. He has focused concentration, just like the Hawk.

I would also like to thank a lot of good golf people for their help:

Joe Jeroski, former CPGA professional, and the ever-helpful John Downie for sharing their Ben Hogan collections.

The managers of Point Grey, Capilano, Marine Drive, and Shaughnessy Golf and Country Clubs for their cooperation.

The Archives specialists at Vancouver Planetarium, and the University of BC, and Vancouver Library's Special Collections.

Mike Manson, archivist for the *New York Times*.

Tom McCarthy of The Ben Hogan Collection.

Dorothy Williams of The Golf House and Museum at University Golf Club.

Yvette Reyes of Associated Press library.

Special thanks to Gerry Kitson, former CPGA professional, who read the third draft, and to Des Dwyer for his insights.

I thank Kevin Riley for his wonderfully delivered stories about Mr. Hogan and the other great players of a bygone age who had so much to do with the evolution of golf.

Colette Miller for her help with communications.

Todd Graves and Doug Brown for finding their old photos.

Grateful thanks to CJ Wilson, Steve Engs, Roy Miller, Lay-up Larry, and Harry Cotter for sharing their caddie stories and their memorabilia with me.

My thanks to artists Bill McLuckie and Peter Burnet.

Jules Alexander, the photographer, who began his career at fifteen taking shots of the up and coming stars and idols in New York like Frank Sinatra, Louis Armstrong, and Duke Ellington. He served as aerial photographer over Europe and the South Pacific during World War II before turning to golf and his fascination and respect for Ben Hogan.

Mike Lilly, a family man who has introduced three sons to golf. A single digit handicap himself, he likes to follow Tiger with a quiet camera.

Derek Thornley and Alvie Thompson two CPGA club professionals who remember their Hogan years fondly.

Photographer Bayne Stanley and CPGA models Wayne Hong and Matt Lister.

And, finally Mark Weinstein of Skyhorse Publishing for a masterful overview.

Ben Hogan holds the PGA Champions trophy won at Norwood Hills St. Louis during a banner season in 1948.

BIBLIOGRAPHY

Books:

Alexander, Jules. *Classic Photographs of the Great Ben Hogan*. In *The Hogan Mystique,* by Martin Davis. Greenwich: American Golfer Inc., 1994.

Andrisani, John. *The Hogan Way*. New York: HarperCollins, 2004.

Bertrand, Tom, and Printer Bowler. *The Secret of Hogan's Swing*. Hoboken: John Wiley & Sons, Inc., 2006.

Davis, Martin. *Ben Hogan: The Man Behind the Mystique*. Greenwich: American Golfer Inc., 2002.

Dobson, James. *Ben Hogan: An American Life*. New York: Doubleday, 2004.

Frost, Mark. *The Match*. New York: Hyperion Books, 2007.

"Golf." *New York Times Encyclopedia of Sports*. Volume 5. New York: Arno Press, 1979.

Hardy, Jim, and John Andrisani. *The Plane Truth for Golfers*. New York: McGraw-Hill, 2005.

Hogan, Ben. *Ben Hogan's Five Lessons: The Modern Fundamentals of Golf*. New York: Simon and Schuster, 1957.

Hogan, Ben. *Power Golf*. New York: A. S. Barnes, 1948.

Leadbetter, David, with Lorne Rubenstein. *The Fundamentals of Hogan*. New York: Doubleday, 2000.

Minni, Scott. *Smash and Carve Golf: The Art of Ball Striking*. New York: Smash and Carve Golf, 1999.

Palmer, Arnold, and James Dobson. *A Golfer's Life*. New York: Ballantine Books, 1999.

Sampson, Curt. *Hogan*. New York: Broadway Books, 1997.

Sinnette, Calvin. *Forbidden Fairways*. Chelsea: Sleeping Bear Press, 1998.

Skyzinski, Rich. *The Quotable Hogan*. Nashville: TowleHouse, 2001.

Thomas, Bob. *Ben Hogan's Secret*. New York: MacMillan Publishing Company, 1997.

Vasquez, Jody. *Afternoons With Mr. Hogan*. New York: Gotham Books, 2005.

Woods, Tiger. *Tiger Woods—How I Play Golf*. New York: Warner Books, 2001.

Magazines:

Golf Digest. March 1994. Guy Yocom. Ben Hogan's Secret. P 53.

Golf Digest. December 1995. David Owen. Moe Knows What Nobody Knows. P 31.

GolfStyle. Summer 2007. Ted Hunt. A Curse Most Cruel. P 124.

Life. August 8 1955. Ben Hogan. This Is My Secret. P 61.

Sports Illustrated. March 1957. H. Wind, A. Ravielli. Ben Hogan Modern Fundamentals. P 16.

Failure Magazine. July 17, 2000. Jason Zasky. The Greatest Golfer the World Has Never Known. P 7.

INDEX